P9-DTS-404

DATE DUE

DEC 2 03			

DEMCO 38-296

U.S. Economic Policy Toward Africa

U.S. Economic Policy Toward Africa

Jeffrey Herbst

COUNCIL ON FOREIGN RELATIONS PRESS

NEW YORK

COUNCIL ON FOREIGN RELATIONS BOOKS

Library of Congress Cataloguing-in-Publication Data

Herbst, Jeffrey Ira.
    U.S. economic policy toward Africa   / Jeffrey Herbst.
    p. cm.
    Includes bibliographical references.
    ISBN 0-87609-121-4 : $12.95
    1. Africa–Foreign Relations–United States. 2. United States–Foreign Relations–Africa. 3. Africa–Foreign Relations–1960- 4. United States–Foreign Relations–1989- I. Title.
DT38.7.H47   1992   92-14959
327.7306–dc20   CIP

92   93   94   95   EB   7   6   5   4   3   2   1

(*Cover Design: Whit Vye*)

CONTENTS

Acknowledgments

I am grateful to the Council on Foreign Relations for convening a study group to help me while writing this book, which has been published with the support of The Ford Foundation. Pauline Baker, Deborah Brautigam, Steve Brent, Tom Callaghy, L. Gray Cowan, Ravi Gulhati, Omutunde Johnson, Joan Nelson, Alison Rosenberg, Steve Weissman, and Jerry Wolgin all provided valuable comments on earlier drafts of this manuscript. I am also grateful to Henry Bienen, John Harbeson, and Donald Rothchild for their insightful suggestions and to Elizabeth Hart for research assistance. My greatest thanks go to Michael Clough who prompted me to write this book and whose comments and questions forced me to strengthen my work considerably.

Introduction

Across the African continent, dozens of countries have begun adopting reforms aimed at fundamentally altering the way their economies function. Sparked in part by the revolutions in Central Europe, many African countries are now also trying to dismantle their authoritarian governments, and some are beginning the difficult process of political liberalization. These hopeful steps, however, are being taken in the context of catastrophic economic decline. Per capita incomes, already low by the late 1970s, declined at an annual rate of 1 percent across the continent during the 1980s.[1] If current trends continue, Africa by the next century will be even more impoverished, with deteriorating social conditions, less food, greater energy shortages, and more unemployment. In addition, if the economic slide is not reversed, there is probably no chance of widespread democratization in Africa.

The United States has a clear interest in the success of African economic and political reform. There has been controversy, however, over what steps the United States should take, especially in its aid programs, to help the countries south of the Sahara move toward more open markets and freer political systems. The stakes are high, especially for Africans themselves, but also for the international community which, since 1980, has committed a total of $27 billion to Africa in aid conditioned on economic and political reform.[2] Given the opportunities and the dangers inherent in reform, there is now more than ever a need for nuanced American policies that can realistically address the difficult problems that Africa faces.

American aid policies toward Africa over the last three decades have often been severely affected by the strategic imperatives of the cold war.[3] Since geopolitical concerns, rather than African realities, were what interested top policy-makers, actual aid programs were seldom the result of a coherent, long-term vision. Rather, American assistance policy often enthusiastically embraced the fad of the moment, only to slowly renounce the initiative in light of the accumulated evidence of failure. In addition to being distracted by the Cold War, part of the problem has simply been a rather difficult learning process of what works and what does not in Africa.

After a review of the evolution of American aid policy, this book will outline the key elements of a successful American foreign assistance program for the 1990s. Using this framework, a series of critical issues that policymakers must confront will be reviewed: how to measure success during economic reform; the role of the African state; and the distributional consequences of economic reform programs and the debt problem. Finally, the problematic relationship between political and economic reform will be examined.

While the political and economic reforms demanded by the United States and other donors are politically difficult, most African countries are stable enough to at least consider how to revamp their fundamental institutions. There is, however, a set of African countries that have essentially stopped functioning (for example, Somalia and Liberia) where the international community's main goal is to prevent mass famine and further widespread violence. Obviously, reform of fundamental institutions is largely a moot issue in these countries. Therefore, this book will concentrate on those countries where reform is at least on the agenda. Indeed, a central aim of U.S. policy in the 1990s will be to help those countries where reform is still possible avoid the spiral of decline that will make anything but disaster relief unimaginable.

1

THE EVOLUTION OF U.S. FOREIGN ASSISTANCE POLICY TOWARD AFRICA

As the postcolonial period ends in Africa, it is important to review official American opinion about Africa during the period. In a prescient 1955 memo to the secretary of state, Assistant Secretary of State of Near Eastern, South Asian, and African Affairs George V. Allen noted that American interests in Africa were "real but limited." Trade and investment with Africa were significant; they paled, however, in comparison to American economic ties with other regions, in part because the colonial powers dominated Africa's economies. While Allen stated that American involvement with Africa would increase after colonialism ended, he did not believe that the United States would come to view Africa in a fundamentally different light in the short term. Indeed, he argued that, since economic assistance would remain limited, "we can assume that whatever the goals of United States policy may be with respect to this part of the Continent, our means to achieve these goals will be inadequate." More attention, however, should be devoted to Africa and "our policy must be based as much on the potentials of Africa as its present condition."[1] For the last thirty-five years, the United States has struggled with expectations that outstrip available resources while anticipating a bright African future that is always just a few years away.

In the flurry of excitement that greeted African independence, U.S. economic assistance, as pictured in Figure 1, did increase significantly. From virtually nothing in 1960, U.S. aid increased to $1.3 billion (1989 dollars) in 1962. American expectations toward Africa were still extremely

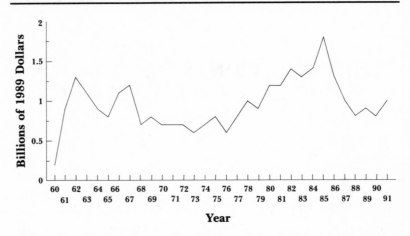

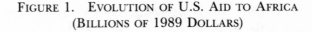

Sources: U.S. Congress, House, *Background Materials on Foreign Assistance* (Washington, D.C.: Government Printing Office, 1989) and *USAID, U.S. Overseas Loans and Grants* (Washington, D.C.: AID, 1990).

FIGURE 1.   EVOLUTION OF U.S. AID TO AFRICA
(BILLIONS OF 1989 DOLLARS)

guarded. In a 1961 memo by the Policy Planning Council, African experts noted that the extremely small size of many African countries foreclosed the possibility of any real autonomous domestic economic development. Should these countries try to industrialize, they argued, "scarce resources will tend to be misdirected into parallel and overlapping investments; and the possibilities of attracting private capital from abroad will be reduced." They suggested that American foreign policy should be devoted largely to promoting regional economic integration so that economies of scale could be achieved through relatively large markets.[2]

Throughout the 1960s, American officials repeatedly suggested that the United States should downplay bilateral foreign aid in favor of regional assistance. For instance, the Clay Commission argued that U.S. assistance should be confined to multilateral programs.[3] There was a continuing push within the burgeoning foreign assistance community, however, to establish bilateral aid missions. In an important 1966 report, Ambassador Edward M. Korry argued that the United States should retain a presence in some countries but that bilateral assistance should be phased out where the United States was not the major source of assistance.[4] He argued that "we cannot pretend to conduct economic development programs in 33 countries."[5]

As Table 1 indicates, while there was a consensus on directing aid to a relatively small number of countries, U.S. policy in practice was moving in precisely the opposite direction. Part of the reason for the diffusion of aid resources was the utility that foreign assistance had in promoting U.S. foreign policy goals during the Cold War. In order to gain United Nations votes and project influence, it was important to have an aid presence in as many countries as possible even if the spread of resources severely limited the usefulness of the money given.

Kennedy and Johnson administration officials also confronted other problems which would bedevil their successors

TABLE 1. NUMBER OF SUB-SAHARAN AFRICAN COUNTRIES
RECEIVING AID

Year	Number of African Countries Receiving Aid
1960	18
1965	35
1970	35
1975	42
1980	46
1985	46
1990	46

Source: USAID, *U.S. Overseas Loans & Grants and Assistance from International Organizations* (Washington, D.C.: USAID, various years).

in ensuing decades. In particular, because African development had proceeded so slowly, officials in the 1960s argued that "we should recognize the chances are great that the performance of the recipient country in carrying out its development plans may fall below what we would consider satisfactory." They also noted "it may be extremely difficult in such circumstances, having once made a commitment, to hold back on it [aid] without causing serious friction, even though we may have made it unmistakably clear that the commitment was contingent on satisfactory performance."[6]

There was thus an early awareness of just how difficult it would be to condition aid on economic performance. Officials recommended that they be allowed to commit money beyond the current fiscal year, thereby indicating to recipient governments that the money was available as long as they pursued reasonably effective economic policies. In fact, the only money that the United States was able to disburse quickly was what became known as Economic Support Funds (formerly called Security Support Assistance), a budget line originally intended to aid strategic allies. Other accounts became, if anything, more difficult to commit and spend.

The philosophy of American aid during the 1960s reflected the prevailing political concerns and economic theories of the time. Although Africa was relatively unimportant from a strategic perspective, the relatively minor U.S. economic and political interests meant that cold war concerns often dominated American policy toward the continent. U.S. leaders often only became engaged in African issues in order to deny the Soviet Union important strategic advantages. As David D. Newsom noted in his review of U.S. policy toward the countries south of the Sahara, "The East-West confrontation appeared to assure the greatest justification for broad-based and long-term support for an African policy."[7] In good part, geopolitical concerns would determine the overall level of resources devoted to Africa and which countries would be primary recipients.

Economically, aid was seen largely as a way of meeting the gaps developing countries experienced in financing either domestic investment or foreign imports. In particular, the construction of an adequate physical infrastructure was a prime goal of aid policy because, especially in Africa, capital stocks were so low. A fairly direct causal relationship was assumed between the total level of capital investment in a developing country and its overall development. Given the focus on capital flows, much less attention was devoted to the domestic policies of African countries, although U.S. foreign policy has always been publicly committed to promoting private investment. In addition, general development thinking in the 1960s did not devote significant attention to the enhancement of human capital or specific poverty alleviation measures. Indeed, of all of AID's regional bureaus, the Africa section had been the most insistent that aid be concentrated on large-scale infrastructure projects, especially in the areas of transportation and water.[8]

In the early 1970s, U.S. foreign aid policy underwent a major evolution. There had been growing dissatisfaction within the political establishment with foreign aid in general because it was perceived as not helping the poorest people in the Third World. Rather, the "trickle down" model of development, which featured the construction of capital intensive projects, was seen as contributing to the worsening of poverty in many countries. It should be noted that at least part of this new concern was generated not by real evaluations of aid programs but simply because poverty within the United States had been a priority for some time, and there has been a tendency to transfer U.S. domestic concerns to American aid policy.[9] As a result, Congress passed the New Directions legislation in 1973, which sought to fundamentally alter the approach of American aid policy. The primary emphasis of future aid was placed on meeting the basic needs of the rural poor majority in Africa and other developing countries.

The New Directions strategy was only slowly adopted by the aid bureaucracy, in part because the congressional legislation was so ambiguous. Throughout the 1970s, however, the momentum behind the New Directions approach increased. After President Carter's election in 1976, the focus on the poor was further emphasized. In adopting this approach, the United States was in accord with much of official thinking of the time, especially the basic human needs philosophy espoused by the World Bank and the International Labour Organization.

The legislation adopted by Congress changed foreign assistance strategy in many ways. There was supposed to be a shift from capital intensive projects to projects focusing on the welfare of the poor. However, the New Directions legislation also demanded that the United States not be concerned with the long-term viability of national markets. Rather, aid officials were asked to focus on local projects that helped as many poor people as possible. The new policy directives therefore represented a 180-degree change from previous efforts which sought to have the United States work more at the regional level. Although in 1966 Ambassador Korry had proposed concentrating aid in a few African countries, by the 1980s, the U.S. Agency for International Development (AID) had missions in twenty-three African countries and a presence of some kind in close to two dozen more.

Aid officials recognized that the kind of development it hoped would help the poor would also require economic policies that promoted saving and investment, widened access to resources and employment, and altered fundamental institutions such as land tenure. Indeed, AID argued that "without such reforms, the intended results of other efforts to benefit the poor can be more than offset." While endorsing the need for structural reforms, AID was much less clear on outlining what changes it would actually ask Third World countries to implement.[10] Goler Butcher, AID's assistant administrator for Africa, noted in 1979, "We have tended in the last few years to look at our problems in what I might call a microeconomic context without looking at it with respect to the situation of the whole country."[11]

The 1980s would see a fundamental change in the philosophy of U.S. foreign aid to Africa and the rest of the Third World. The election of Ronald Reagan forced the entire aid bureaucracy to rethink its approach to economic policy, especially regarding the state as an economic actor. The Reagan administration's suspicion of the state's role in economic development would have important ramifications for Africa for two reasons. First, African countries, irrespective of pronounced ideology, had adopted policies which encouraged state ownership of a significant portion of the formal economy. Many countries also had extensive systems of subsidies, wage and price controls, and foreign exchange regulations that stifled the private sector. Second, both the infrastructure projects and basic needs programs that the aid bureaucracy had championed in the 1960s and 1970s directed almost all funds through the state while slighting the private sector.

At the same time, there was a growing consensus in the aid community worldwide that the kind of project approach exemplified by the basic human needs philosophy would not have substantial impact because the policy environment of African countries was so poor. For example, it would not be very helpful if AID built clinics if an African government did not have the funds for staff and supplies. In an important early policy statement, Frank Ruddy, Butcher's successor at AID, said that it must be made clear that African development would

> in the end be determined by African governments, not donors. For instance, agricultural pricing, policy on parastatals, credit policy, foreign exchange policy, and budget policy to name a few are all domestic issues to be resolved by governments in response to their individual needs. Unless these policies encourage development, the contribution of donors is simply an expensive form of temporizing.[12]

Much of this policy thrust originated in the World Bank's influential 1981 report, *Accelerated Development in Sub-Saharan Africa,* which placed a substantial portion of the blame for Africa's poor economic performance on policies that African countries had adopted. Administration officials constantly cited the World Bank's report in justifying their own change in policy, a pattern which would continue throughout the 1980s.

In addition to the intellectual revolution, the Reagan administration's vision of U.S. interests in Africa differed fundamentally from the Carter administration's vision. In its 1980 discussion paper, *Sub-Saharan Africa and the United States,* the State Department noted that U.S. efforts to aid Africa "reflect a high degree of interdependence between Africa and America."[13] The Reagan administration abandoned the rhetoric of mutual interdependence and focused much more on the need for African countries to promote reforms and on U.S. security concerns. In one of the clearest linkages of Africa's economic problems to the cold war, Assistant Secretary of State for African Affairs Chester Crocker argued that promoting the abandonment of statist and anti-market policies, "would constitute a major American success and a significant defeat for our adversaries' influence in the third world."[14]

The Reagan administration's position was also driven partially by the fact that Africa was becoming less important to the United States. Indeed, although U.S. trade with Africa was always low, it actually declined further during the 1980s. In 1983, for instance, U.S. exports to Africa amounted to 2.7 percent of total U.S. exports and imports from Africa accounted for 5.5 percent of total imports. By 1989, exports to Africa accounted for only 1.4 percent of total American exports and imports from Africa for only 3.0 percent of the total value of goods the United States purchased from the rest of the world.[15] The reduction in economic ties seems to have come about because of U.S. sanctions imposed on South Africa, the decline in oil prices, and the general economic crisis that gripped the continent throughout the 1980s. Similarly, U.S. investment in Africa is extremely low. In 1990, only .46 percent of total U.S. direct investment abroad was in sub-Saharan Africa.[16]

Despite the rhetoric on the need for changes in domestic African economies, during most of the 1980s, security interests prohibited American officials from pursuing economic reform in a dedicated manner. The United States continued to provide aid to Numeri in Sudan, Doe in Liberia, Siad Barre in Somalia, and Mobutu in Zaire, among others, although it was obvious that none of these leaders was serious about reform. Indeed, in their review of aid allocation patterns, World Bank officials Ravi Gulhati and Raj Nallari found that political events had a major effect on U.S. aid allocations in Eastern and Southern Africa in the 1970s and 1980s. Developments related to the Cold War, such as the 1980 Base Rights agreement with Kenya and Somalia's switch out of the Soviet camp greatly affected aid allocations. As a result, not surprisingly, U.S. aid allocations were far less oriented toward development than those of West Germany or the United Kingdom (although more development-oriented than French or Japanese aid).[17] Provision of aid on a political basis, especially to governments which were obviously dysfunctional (for example, Somalia and Zaire), served to make other African countries cynical about the true intentions of the United States and especially about the American commitment to reform. More generally, the political benefits provided by aid forced AID to continue its widely dispersed operations rather than concentrating on countries that demonstrated their intent to reform.

As Figure 1 suggests, American aid to Africa increased after 1981 in real terms. The peak was hit in 1985, but the total for that year, as well as for 1986, is artificially inflated because it includes food aid donated to Ethiopia during the famine. In the late 1980s, aid to Africa in real terms declined significantly. Figure 2 suggests that the reason for the decrease

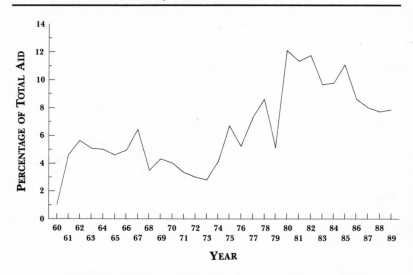

Sources: U.S. Congress, House, *Background Materials on Foreign Assistance* (Washington, D.C.: Government Printing Office, 1989) and *USAID, U.S. Overseas Loans and Grants* (Washington, D.C.: AID, 1990).

FIGURE 2.   AID TO AFRICA AS A PERCENTAGE OF TOTAL AID

in real aid was reductions in the total aid budget. Indeed, the Reagan administration increased the percentage of American aid going to Africa to historically high levels. Even in the early 1980s, when Africa's share of the total U.S. aid budget was high, it still amounted to less than 13 percent of the total money given. Thus, while Washington's expectations of what aid should accomplish increased dramatically, there was only a marginal increase in total funding. As had been predicted in the 1960s, expectations had outstripped resources.

The major economic initiative of the Reagan administration toward Africa was presented to Congress in 1984. The Economic Policy Initiative (EPI) was supposed to be a five-year $500-million effort that would direct "funds toward countries that can establish a suitable comprehensive economic policy framework. Such a framework would need to go beyond the immediate macroeconomic stabilization measures and include sectoral policies conducive to growth and longer run development." The funds were not committed to any one nation and were supposed to be given on a no-year basis in order to increase AID's flexibility in asking for and funding reforms.[18] Of course, AID's request that it be allowed to give foreign assistance in such a flexible manner reflected the organization's long-held beliefs made clear in the 1960s.

AID's policy initiative was approved, although, not surprisingly, at lower levels than the agency had asked. AID had projected the program to cost $500 million through fiscal year (FY) 1989, but only $255 million was actually authorized and the initiative came to be called the African Economic Policy Reform Program (AEPRP). The underfunding of the initiative was in and of itself an excellent example of the gap between intentions and resources that has long afflicted American foreign aid policy.

In 1988, foreign assistance toward Africa underwent a further evolution when the Development Fund for Africa (DFA) was created out of already existing budget lines. Economic support funds in all but eight strategically important countries were folded into the development account. As a result, funding to countries demonstrating a commitment to reform (mainly, Ghana, Guinea, Madagascar, Malawi, Tanzania, and Uganda) increased by over 80 percent. Aid to poor performers such as Liberia, Somalia, Zambia, and Zaire decreased markedly although primarily because of congressional concerns over human rights.[19] The DFA money, untied, quick disbursing, and able to be committed two years in advance, was hailed by AID as being especially appropriate to promote policy reform.

The DFA reflected the increasing emphasis of overall U.S. aid policy on economic reform. The ability of the United States to redirect money from Monrovia, Mogadishu, and Kinshasa, despite the fact that the United States had long-standing security relations with each of those regimes, also reflected the increasing freedom of the United States to introduce other concerns into its post–Cold War aid policy. Indeed, the fact that the United States stood aside during 1990 and 1991 while regimes fell in Liberia, Chad, and Somalia—governments that it invested heavily in and that were once considered important—shows how little Washington is now captive to strategic interests in Africa. Correspondingly, the American interest in pursuing reform in order to benefit Africans has become much more credible.

Aid to Africa increased markedly during the early 1990s. Due in good part to efforts by the Congressional Black Caucus, DFA has doubled in three years. The sharp rise in assistance to Africa, at the same time that the United States was providing significant resources to the new Central European democracies, showed that the United States would not automatically abandon Africa despite the fact that aid to that marginalized continent could not be justified by security concerns. Of course, U.S. aid to Africa will not increase so much in the future that America could have a decisive effect on reform efforts.

Intellectually, by the end of the 1980s, American policy had shifted dramatically from the New Directions approach first enacted in 1973, but there were still many in Congress who did not agree with AID's new emphasis on policy-based reform. As the Congressional Research Service noted, "The extent to which aid resources should focus on promoting growth through reliance on private entrepreneurship and market mechanisms as opposed to strengthening the resources of the dispossessed remains a key issue for debate."[20] Indeed, a recent congressional investigation of U.S.–supported economic reforms in Ghana and Senegal produced a strong indictment of these programs noting that, "despite rising per capita growth, structural adjustment has produced little enduring poverty-alleviation and certain policies have worked against the poor."[21]

As a result, U.S. aid policy still suffers from an abundance of goals in comparison to the financial resources available, even with the higher aid levels of the last few years. For instance, the foreign aid appropriations legislation for 1991 declared in part that the purpose of DFA was "to help the poor majority of men and women in sub-Saharan Africa to participate in a process of long-term development through economic growth that is equitable, participatory, environmentally sustainable, and self-reliant."[22] Less attention seems to have been given to the problem that some of these goals might be contradictory or that there was little chance of Africa making progress on so many fronts at once. Congress has also mandated specific levels of funding for social programs such as family planning and health and for the environment. It is, of course, ironic that just as the Cold War is ending and political calculations are receding in the determination of aid policy, whole new issues threaten to distract American policymakers from the central problem of promoting growth and education.

Given that U.S. aid policy is not grounded in firm congressional support and is vulnerable to sudden swings in American electoral politics, there is a need to develop sound policies now that will serve the United States through the 1990s. American policy must be rethought so that it is more in accord with the level of resources the United States is willing to commit. There is also a need to address the concerns of other constituencies who believe that the policy reform focus of American policy is misguided. Finally, Washington must convince Africans that the United States has established a firm set of priorities and that they will not face a whole new set of demands at some later date if they begin to take Washington's advice now.

The United States and Other Foreign Aid Donors

The United States has never been a significant aid contributor to Africa. In the late 1950s, American officials recognized that the colonial powers would play a substantially more important role in Africa than the United States for some time to come. Indeed, U.S. aid to Africa is only 9 percent of total aid given to the continent by all bilateral donors, while the United States accounts for 17 percent of all bilateral aid given worldwide. The recent increase in American aid meant that, for 1990, only France gave more money to Africa among the bilateral donors. In recent years, however, France, Germany, Italy, and Japan all usually donated more assistance to sub-Saharan Africa.[23]

The U.S. contribution to Africa's development is even less impressive once the multilateral organizations are included. The World Bank and its soft loan window, the International Development Association, account for a significant percentage of the total overseas development assistance (ODA) devoted to Africa. The World Bank group gave 11 percent of all aid to Africa in 1990 compared to the American contribution of 6 percent. The European Development Fund, the aid arm of the European Community, also accounted for 9 percent of all aid given to Africa.[24] Indeed, during the 1980s, the multilateral organizations responded to Africa's economic crisis with an unprecedented increase in financing. For instance, the World Bank created the $1.2 billion Special Facility for Sub-Saharan Africa in 1985 and later established the Special Program of Assistance to help debt-distressed countries in Africa. Donors pledged $5.8 billion to promote structural adjustment in Africa through this program between 1988 and 1990. Although its loans are not counted as aid, the IMF also became significantly more important to Africa, especially since most sub-Saharan countries had not availed themselves of IMF financing facilities in the 1960s and 1970s. For instance, the IMF authorized members to make cumulative purchases outside of the special facilities of 500 percent of the member's quotas in 1981, significantly increasing the resources available to Africa. The IMF also created a special structural adjustment facility for low-income, primarily African countries in 1985. This facility rechannels IMF trust fund receipts to provide highly concessional medium-term assistance.[25] Of course, the fact that the multilaterals were dramatically increasing their funds to Africa at the same time that the United States was experiencing such budget difficulties served as a powerful reminder that the United States was becoming less and less important to Africa's overall financing.

The World Bank in particular also exerts influence in other ways. Beginning in the early 1970s, while Robert McNamara was president, the World Bank began to become more important in setting the intellectual agenda for African development. McNamara's advocacy of the basic human needs approach had a substantial impact on U.S. foreign aid policy throughout the 1970s. The World Bank's intellectual dominance became even more noticeable in the 1980s when it changed the development agenda in Africa by focusing much more on the impact of African governments' own domestic policies on prospects for growth. As noted above, American officials repeatedly used the World Bank's pivotal 1981 report and subsequent publications in justifying their own policy changes to Congress. By the late 1980s, it was clear that the United States was contributing relatively little to new thinking in Africa, being largely content to piggy-back on the World Bank's thinking.

The multilateral organizations' intellectual dominance is due in good part to their substantial advantages over AID and every other bilateral aid organization. The World Bank is able to employ thousands of development specialists at very high salaries. Its economists are among the best in the world, and they are encouraged to both produce and be involved in a tremendous amount of independent research. Although the World Bank's concentration of personnel in Washington presents some real problems, the fact that it possesses the largest aggregation of people interested in development in the world makes it the acknowledged intellectual leader in the field. The IMF, while keeping a much lower profile than the World Bank, also possesses significant resources and is seen by all governments as a powerful economic actor in its own right and an important commentator on the international economy.

Given its extremely limited funds, AID cannot hope to compete with the World Bank in generating research. In addition, as a decentralized organization with many people in the field, AID does not have much of an intellectual presence in development economics. This is not a criticism of AID personnel, most of whom are dedicated and extremely competent professionals, as much as an observation that the resources available and the structure of the different organizations naturally determines how much of the intellectual agenda each will set.

The United States has dealt with the conflict of having ambitious goals for Africa but being able to contribute only a declining share of resources to Africa in several ways. First, AID argues, correctly, that of the bilateral donors only it has the economic expertise, interest, and prestige to provide "substantive advice on the reform process." Therefore, it plays an important role in contributing to the effectiveness of policy reforms. In addition, the United States seeks to push the debate on policy forward because it is the "most consistent and vigorous proponent of free market solutions to economic problems."[26]

The United States, as the major contributor to the multilaterals, has a role in determining the World Bank and IMF policies toward Africa. In particular, the United States was successful in increasing the percentage of the IDA lending to Africa during the 1980s. This redirection occurred even as the United States was unilaterally reducing its commitment to International Development Association (IDA). The U.S. efforts in IDA can be read as trying to get other countries to contribute more to Africa through an organization that the United States had more control over, and more faith in, than the other Western nations' bilateral aid policies.

As with its own bilateral aid, the United States may not have used its position in the multilateral agencies to comprehensively advance the cause of reform in Africa. Now, given the new freedom that American policymakers possess in the post–cold war world, it will be possible to restructure American aid directly and have an influence on multilateral assistance so that these funds can more effectively promote reform in Africa. The following chapters detail how the United States can reform its structures and policies in an effective manner.

2

A REFORMULATED AID POLICY

A revised aid policy toward Africa would have three elements. First, aid to Africa would be concentrated in a few countries that have demonstrated their commitment to reform. The presumption should be against supporting aid operations in a country unless there is a demonstrative effort to reform fundamental economic institutions. AID would then only operate in a dozen African countries, or roughly half the number it currently has missions in. As a result, the average amount of assistance in the countries that AID continues to operate in would increase. Chapter 3 discusses in detail how AID should evaluate the effectiveness of the reform programs in African countries.

AID needs to consolidate its operations. In many ways, AID has the worst of all worlds at present. It is demanding large policy changes so that it must, as officials have noted since the 1960s, establish significant credibility with African governments. On the other hand, due to the Cold War and previous efforts to provide basic human needs assistance, AID has commitments in a very large number of countries, which prevents it from having a significant policy impact anywhere. U.S. assistance is currently provided to over forty countries and AID has designated twenty-three countries as priority under DFA. As Table 2 documents, the geographic dispersal of resources has meant that AID devotes less and less of its total resources to the top recipients of assistance. Indeed, some of the countries that AID has decided to focus on because of their supposed commitment to reform suggests that the agency has not been forced to be discriminating enough in its allocations. For example, despite all evidence to the contrary, Zaire was until recently considered a Category I

TABLE 2. PERCENTAGE OF AID RECEIVED BY TOP FIVE
RECIPIENT COUNTRIES

Year	Percentage
1960	86.0
1965	57.9
1970	61.7
1975	41.2
1980	39.2
1985	42.6
1990	31.1

Source: USAID, *U.S. Overseas Loans & Grants and Assistance from International Organizations* (Washington, D.C.: USAID, various years).

country, the definition of which includes "a demonstrated commitment to sound and/or improved economic policies."[1] Ambassador Korry's warning that a coherent policy could not be conducted simultaneously in dozens of countries was prescient.

Not surprisingly, given AID's limited analytic resources in Washington and the large number of countries it services in Africa, U.S. aid tends to be incremental in nature. The current year's aid commitments can usually be explained by examining the amounts allocated in preceding years.[2] Such an incremental approach works against rewarding countries that are reforming because most countries will have good reason to believe that the United States will not respond quickly to domestic policy reforms. The AEPRP, which is supposed to allow AID to target money to a few countries that demonstrate significant commitment to reform, was only allocated $60 million of the $800 million that AID requested for the 1991–1992 fiscal year.[3] Thus, AID's dispersed structure aggravates the gap between intentions and resources.

As a result of the aid policies of the United States and other donors, the cost of economic failure for African leaders has not been high enough. What is striking about Africa is that in at least one way it is far too stable: governments can stay in power despite years of economic decline. Leaders such as Julius Nyerere in Tanzania, Kenneth Kaunda in Zambia, or Joseph Mobutu in Zaire survived for decades despite the enormous economic declines their countries experienced. Too often, African leaders have been able to shift failure to the politically silent rural populations and continue to rule no matter how their economies fare. An American policy that explicitly diverted resources from poor reformers would increase the costs of poor economic performance to African leaders.

Also, a deliberate policy of concentrating assistance would provide a definitive break with the old, Cold War policies. African leaders realize that the end of the Cold War will mean that they will increasingly be judged on how they perform economically. The presence, however, of slow-moving, incremental bureaucracies like AID, which are dedicated to dispersing assistance to a relatively large number of countries, may dilute the message that success at economic reform is the major criteria for aid. The recently approved increase in American resources going to Africa may only aggravate this problem. Concentrating resources in fewer countries would give the United States far greater credibility in demanding policy reforms from recipients of its aid.

Finally, Africa needs demonstrative economic successes. Much of the current opposition to stabilization and structural adjustment in Africa is not due to an allegiance to socialism but to a pervasive fear that Africans cannot rely on the market to succeed. There is a belief that African economies are too different for traditional measures to provoke success; many on the continent also believe that they cannot compete on the world market. These fears will remain salient as long as no country in Africa is an unquestionable success. In East Asia, Japan provided an important precedent for policymakers in many countries who argued that their countries could also succeed if they adopted the necessary policies.

The other East Asian countries did not simply duplicate the Japanese model; indeed, their economic policies actually vary considerably. Japan, however, served as a benchmark for Asia and demonstrated the rewards of tough policies and appropriate technologies.[4] Africa needs a similar example if leaders who are advocating tough reforms are to have credibility.

Thus, aid should be concentrated to increase the possibility that at least some countries will break out of the old pattern of stagnation and serve as exemplary models for the rest of the continent. Those who criticize the United States and the World Bank for providing large amounts of aid to early reformers like Ghana miss an important element of promoting overall reform in Africa. Of course, demonstrative success in Africa would also do more than anything else to strengthen the domestic constituencies in the United States in favor of increased economic assistance to Africa.

This is not to say that countries that, at a later date, might begin serious economic reform would be abandoned. The United States gives only a small percentage of total aid to Africa. Other donors could easily step in to provide aid if any countries outside the small set selected for aid by the United States begin seriously to implement reform.

Second, the United States must make a credible commitment to the promotion of economic reform as its central priority for the foreseeable future. U.S. policy has been subject to frequent changes in priority due to developments inside the United States or because of changing strategic concerns. If African countries are going to risk the difficult process of economic reform, however, they must understand that, while the United States will be tough in its demands, it will not change its priorities in the future. This kind of commitment is particularly difficult for the United States to make given the open nature of the foreign policy process. Chapter 5 discusses one way to ensure the credibility of U.S. aid policy: change the multilateral institutions' debt policy so that African economies have a chance to grow. Such a reform would send a powerful signal that the United States was firmly committed to promoting reform and willing to change fundamental international practices to help African countries in significant ways.

The third aspect of a reformulated aid policy is that the focus of assistance above all else would be on promoting growth and building human capital. American policy must constantly stress that the overwhelming priority for African countries is to enhance the prospects for economic growth and education. This is a simple message but one that the United States, because of all the other priorities that have impinged on aid policy, has sometimes been poor at communicating. Economic growth provides the resources to meet other priorities and is thus absolutely essential. Shortages of trained manpower and a large illiterate population are enormous drags on development even if prices are right and all the structural reforms are made. In addition, studies suggest that the effect of education on household welfare is strong.[5]

A clear statement of growth and education as the key priorities for Africa is vitally needed. Traditionally, much of U.S. aid was perceived as being linked to Washington's strategic objectives. Also, Congress and many other special interest groups have sought to promote all kinds of other goals as important parts of American foreign aid. Indeed, as conditionality becomes prevalent in international economic relations, many in the West have demanded that aid be linked to an increasing number of goals that some in the West find attractive. For instance, some have argued that aid should be conditioned on increasing aid to children, while others have argued that foreign assistance should be linked to decreasing military spending.[6] No doubt, environmental conditionality will soon be placed on the agenda by other well-meaning groups. The recent jump in American aid to Africa may encourage the proclivity of the various interest groups to demand increasingly elaborate conditionality.

Suggestions that U.S. foreign assistance be diverted from its primary mission of promoting economic reform are mistaken. If one clear message emerges out of East Asia it is that poor countries must have a long-term fixation with growth. As Chalmers Johnson noted in his study of Japan,

> A state attempting to match the economic achievements of Japan must adopt the same priorities as Japan. It must first of all be a developmental state—and only then a regulatory state, a welfare state, an equality state, or whatever other kind of functional state a society may wish to adopt.[7]

Chapter 4 discusses the future of African economies and analyzes how the United States can promote useful institutional reform to promote growth. The same chapter also discusses why increasing aid to the poor in Africa—a constant theme of many critics of current U.S. policy—would be a mistake. Chapter 6 suggests why the United States should continue to condition aid primarily on economic reform and not tie aid directly to democratization.

To say that the United States should focus on promoting economic growth and building human capital is not to slight other goals that have a legitimate role in U.S. policy. If African countries do not grow, however, there is no chance that other priorities including environmental protection, helping the poor, promoting the roles of women, and fostering democratization will be successfully addressed. To say otherwise is to ignore the lessons of those countries that have managed the difficult task of promoting growth and the example of African countries that continue to deteriorate.

There are many other aspects of any comprehensive foreign aid policy. If American aid were to be more concentrated among fewer successful reformers, if the United States could make a commitment to economic reform for the long term, and if promotion of economic growth and the development of human capital were the unquestioned priorities, aid policy would be dramatically reformed for the better. The following chapters detail some of the implications of a reformulated American aid policy.

3

EVALUATING SUCCESS

If the United States is to concentrate aid among successful reforms, success must be clearly defined. Unfortunately, one of the most difficult aspects of the economic reform programs suggested to Africa by the United States and other donors is that there is little agreement on how to measure their effectiveness. It is particularly surprising, given the consensus that has developed on what is wrong with African countries and what to do about those problems, that no clear expectations exist about how these economies will perform once stabilization and structural adjustment programs have been adopted. The failure to develop a consensus concerning the expected benefits has caused almost constant friction between Western donors, who are enthusiastic about the results of stabilization and structural adjustment, and African leaders, for whom the political costs of the programs are high and the economic benefits limited. After briefly describing the reforms suggested by the United States and other donors, this chapter will examine how these programs have been evaluated to date and suggest a more realistic alternative.

Stabilization and Structural Adjustment Programs

There is now a widespread consensus in the developed countries about what is wrong with African economies. At the most basic level, many African economies suffer from severe imbalances. They import more than they export and have unsustainable external deficits. This imbalance is driven by an overvalued exchange rate, which causes imports to seem artificially inexpensive and makes it unprofitable to export.

Therefore, the IMF has demanded, as part of many stabilization programs, that countries implement large devaluations of their exchange rates. In one study, liberalization and reform of exchange rate regimes were features in more than half of the programs supported by the IMF in Africa between 1980 and 1984.[1] Similarly, government expenditures, fueled by subsidies and losses of state-owned enterprises, have frequently exceeded revenue, resulting in unacceptable government deficits. Of forty-one IMF programs in sub-Saharan Africa between 1980 and 1986, 85 percent put limits on government borrowing and expenditures and almost 90 percent demanded a reduction in the fiscal deficit.[2]

The United States has little to do with the design of stabilization programs, especially in the early stages. The IMF, charged since the end of World War II with helping countries stabilize their economies, has traditionally taken the lead in both designing and funding initial stabilization programs. When an African country signs a standby agreement with the IMF, however, it sends a signal to the international community that it is willing to undertake important economy reforms.

In conjunction with initial stabilization programs, the World Bank, the U.S. government, and other bilateral donors will begin to pressure an African government to undertake other economic reforms. Given that 70 percent of the people in Africa farm, there is usually an immediate emphasis on agriculture. In particular, since many African countries have traditionally underpaid their farmers for both food and export crops, donors pressure countries to raise agricultural producer prices. Reform of agricultural producer pricing has been a major component in over 80 percent of all World Bank Structural Adjustment Loans for Africa that affected agriculture.[3] There has also been a long-term emphasis on improving the entire agrarian infrastructure: rebuilding roads, reconstructing seed and fertilizer delivery systems, and improving extension agencies. If these reforms are not implemented, then it will limit the ability of farmers to respond to the improved prices.

As structural adjustment continues, the World Bank, which technically has lead responsibility among donors to promote long-term changes that promote growth, will suggest a host of other reforms. For example, many African countries allowed their state-owned enterprises to become extremely inefficient, crowding out the private sector. Therefore, reform programs often include provisions to make these corporations more efficient or to privatize them. African countries have frequently implemented a host of other provisions, including price controls and regulation of investment, that are targets of reform programs. Also, due to the spiral of decline that many African countries have undergone, a host of institutions, including the financial sector, the tax system, and many fundamental aspects of the state itself, have to be dramatically reformed if these countries are to have any hope for growth.

The reforms suggested by the developed nations pose enormous political problems for African countries. At the most basic level, cutting subsidies, reducing many government services (schools, clinics, etc.), and increasing the prices of many basic goods dramatically affect the livelihood of their citizens, almost all of whom are already poor by any standard. Especially difficult for these countries is that many of the reforms are directed against the politically important urban populations, who have occasionally rioted when the programs were too onerous. The Numeiri government in Sudan fell due to riots after the announcement of a stabilization program, and reforms in countries such as Zambia, Tunisia, and Côte d'Ivoire were temporarily shelved when the governments involved felt threatened by urban unrest.

The thrust of most African countries' economic programs since independence has been to increase state intervention in order to capture the "commanding heights of the economy." The stabilization and structural adjustment programs demand that governments devolve a significant amount of economic decision-making to the market, automatically increasing the insecurity of national leaders. If African leaders control fewer levers in the economy, they will no longer will be able to reward important political allies. Thus, the programs demanded by the United States and the other donors pose fundamental challenges to the way that African economies and African political systems have operated over the past thirty years.

Given the political challenges that economic reform presents, it is important for African leaders to show their populations that economic reform programs are working. Indeed, the effectiveness of reforms has become crucial, because stabilization and structural adjustment programs remove many of the symbols that African governments had used to gather popular support. Whatever its economic faults, the vague African socialism that many countries adopted after independence provided rituals, icons, and a political vocabulary, around which governments could rally their populations. Economic reform programs diminish many of these symbols, and the World Bank and the IMF do not provide a political vocabulary to accompany their elegant economic logic. Without proof that these programs are effective, governments may have no means of gaining legitimacy.

Measuring the Effectiveness of Reform

Gauging the effectiveness of economic reform programs is difficult. At the most basic level, economic data are so bad in African countries that heroic assumptions have to be made about statistics used in formulating fine gradations in the performance of African countries. In its influential 1981 report, the World Bank noted that estimates for growth of some countries varied tremendously.[4] Many of the statistics most important in the evaluation of economic reform programs can also be manipulated easily by governments desperately in need of continued external finance. For example, more than a few African countries have delayed writing checks for a few days in order to meet IMF targets on budget deficits. Some countries probably keep separate accounts for politically important items to demonstrate to the IMF that they are within the agreed-upon parameters. Thus, the more evaluation measures rely on a few short-term statistics, the more questionable they become.

Ideally, an economic reform program would be judged by comparing it to what would have happened in the country in the absence of the program. In practice, such a comparison is extremely difficult, and advanced econometric tools to try to compare performance against the counterfactual are still being developed.[5] Other means of evaluating reform are problematic at best. For example, studies by the World Bank and the Economic Commission for Africa (ECA) have both tried to compare countries that have adopted economic reform with those that did not. These studies came to differing conclusions. The World Bank, not surprisingly, found that economic reform had a positive impact, while the ECA found that it had a deleterious effect on African countries.[6]

Another possible way of studying the effects of reform programs is to compare a country's performance to the IMF targets agreed to in the standby agreements. For example, IMF officials Justin B. Zulu and Saleh M. Nsouli found that only one-fifth of African countries met the targets set for growth, while only one-half reached their inflation goals and one-third achieved their current accounts target.[7] The problem with this type of evaluation, as the authors note, is that implementation of IMF programs alone will not guarantee achievement of the targets. If the economy is hit with exogenous shocks (for example, a decrease in the price of the major export), the targets will not be reached. Also, even small African economies are complex systems and there is no guarantee that in the short term the measures available to a government will have much effect on macroeconomic aggregates. Even if IMF-suggested measures do not reach their targets, it does not mean that a better program existed for African countries to adopt.

Thus, making judgments concerning the effectiveness of reforms, especially in the short term, is extremely difficult. It is shocking that, despite the fact that dozens of countries in Africa are betting the future of millions of people on the effectiveness of the reform programs and that the developed world is devoting billions of dollars to supporting stabilization and structural adjustment, a consensus has not been reached in even the technical literature on how to judge these programs.

There has been an open political battle between World Bank officials and African leaders concerning the effectiveness of reforms. For example, World Bank officials produced a brief evaluation of reforms in early 1989 claiming that the new programs were working and that the results were visible. African leaders, however, looking at the same data, found much less to be happy about and heavily criticized the World Bank for prematurely evaluating the reforms.[8]

Even if they were to agree on a methodology, African leaders will always be less enamored with the results of economic reform because, if there is an improvement in the macroeconomic aggregates, the figures that the World Bank concentrates on, the vast majority of people in Africa will still be mired in poverty. The World Bank is comparing a reform program's results against past or potential economic performance, while African leaders are comparing the outcome against the political costs they incur. Thus, any estimate of a program's short-term impact will be controversial.

There is good reason to be pessimistic about the impact of economic reform in Africa for years to come. First, most African institutional structures are in such poor condition that they can only slowly adopt economic reform programs. Simply to eliminate the host of economic distortions that African states have incurred will take comprehensive reform programs years, and governments may not have the manpower to staff these programs. Second, African economies are so fragile, especially given their large peasant economies and their dependence on one or two exports, that there is little reason to believe that they can grow quickly in the short term. Third, the average African country's economy has declined significantly since 1973. Even if African countries do begin to grow again, they will only slowly be able to reverse the decline they have experienced over the last eighteen years.

Indeed, the World Bank estimates that even if African countries successfully reform their economies and if the world does supply additional funds, most economies on the continent can only expect to grow at a rate of 4 to 5 percent annually.[9] Given population growth rates of 3.1 percent and the need to put significant resources aside as savings in order to fund future investment, most countries will see only minimal increases in consumption in the near future. Since structural adjustment programs seek to redistribute income from the urban to the rural areas, many city residents will see their consumption levels increase only marginally in the short to medium term. Thus, even African governments that perform well will have to wait many years before their citizens see significant benefits from the sacrifices they are being asked to make. The bottom line is that the best many African countries can hope for (assuming a favorable international climate) is that in ten or fifteen years their economies will return to the levels they achieved in the early years after independence in the 1960s.

Simply because the orthodox reform programs will not result in early, significant gains in African economies does not mean that there is an obvious alternative to these programs. Throughout the 1980s aid officials and African governments came to the dual realization that the reform process would be much slower in yielding positive results than originally thought, and that there was no coherent alternative to these reforms. It seems likely that even more obstacles to restoring African economies will be discovered in the future. Therefore, it behooves Western officials to be extremely guarded in portraying the early results of orthodox reform programs. Even outright economic success in Africa will only be slow, and definitive statistical evidence of improvement will take years to accumulate.

The U.S. government faces the same problems when trying to evaluate the economic reform programs that it has now promoted for more than a decade. For example, American officials enthusiastically backed the 1989 World Bank report that created so much friction with African leaders.[10] Also, U.S. administration officials have consistently declared reform programs to be successes, despite the fact that the new policies had only been in place for a short period of time. The classic example is Zaire, which American officials portrayed throughout the 1970s and 1980s as adopting reforms only for the country to continue to spiral downward. Similarly, American officials in the 1980s noted improvements in both Liberia and Sudan, only to have these countries fall apart a few years later. In a less dramatic fashion, other countries have been hailed for their reforms, only for their performances to disappoint at a later date.

American officials are therefore in an extremely difficult position in portraying the results of the reform programs. They want to suggest that Africa is improving both to convince African countries to stay the course and to strengthen the domestic constituency for Africa. It is also difficult to tell Congress, an institution notorious for its inability to focus on the long term, that the aid money being authorized will not have a measurable impact for years, but overselling the reforms that Africa countries are adopting may lead to unrealistic expectations. Expectations that are repeatedly dashed may lead to even more skepticism about Africa's prospects in Congress and the general public and further reduce the constituency for aiding Africa. In the

1980s, there was widespread skepticism that anything positive could happen in countries such as Zaire and Liberia, and this pessimism could easily spread to the rest of Africa.

Fortunately, a better data base is being developed to enable more concrete evaluations of economic reform programs in the future. The World Bank and other UN agencies have provided significant technical assistance to rebuild African statistical services. A large number of in-depth field evaluations of consumption levels and living standards are now being conducted, which should enable African governments and the multilateral institutions to track the actual effect of adjustment programs. These new statistical measures will not be able to indicate if there was a superior policy to the stance that each African country actually undertook, but the new studies are at least a start at developing a more comprehensive picture of the evolution of African economies as they reform.

Focusing on Institutional Change

Given these statistical problems, much more attention should be devoted to changes in institutions, rather than short-term movements in prices or measures of the economy. That is, the success of African countries in altering the fundamental institutional structures that support, and in many cases distort, their economies should be one of the main indicators when judging the success of reforms and selecting the countries the United States should aid. Other statistical measures also will be useful. A perspective that focused on both the institutional changes in the capital and the consumption levels increasingly being measured in the countryside would provide a much more comprehensive and defensible data base by which to judge the progress of African countries in reforming their economies.

Aid agencies trying to evaluate reform naturally look to

statistical measures while slighting institutional reforms. This is unfortunate, because inefficient, distorted, or disintegrating institutions are at the heart of Africa's economic crisis. The World Bank has repeatedly noted that African countries respond slower to economic reforms because there are so many bottlenecks in their economies.[11] For example, potential exporters cannot react to devaluations because the roads leading to their factories have not been maintained; new businesses cannot grow, although restrictive regulations have been eliminated, because there is no credit; or farmers cannot plant more, even though prices have been increased, because the extension structures that are supposed to deliver seeds have collapsed. Focusing on institutional change is therefore concentrating on the most important problems in African economies.

Reforms of basic institutions are also far more politically important than changes in prices. Price reforms, often done by simple proclamation, are easy to implement and just as easy to withdraw. They reflect less a country's earnest commitment to reform than an ad hoc response to donor pressure. Reforming economic institutions is particularly important because it makes reversal of policy much more difficult in the future. Governments could, of course, take back authority that they had given to the market to set prices on goods or foreign exchange, but this would be a much more difficult and obvious step than, for example, letting the fiscal deficit slip beyond the parameters agreed to with the IMF. Changes in actual economic institutions, especially the shedding of decision-making power by the state to the market, indicates a degree of commitment to economic reform that should be rewarded.

A focus on changes in economic institutions is also useful because often it is a very good gauge of the factional politics revolving around economic reform within the leadership of a developing country. For example, a one-time devaluation does not indicate that a government is irrevocably committed to a reform program that promotes exports. Antireform politicians may have only suffered a temporary setback because, as long as the government retains control over the exchange rate, they have not lost the ability to return to past exchange rate policies that encouraged imports. Thus, even though Ghana substantially devalued its currency between 1983 and 1986, strong debate within the country continued over exchange rate policy. Those opposing the devaluations knew that as long as government set the exchange rate administratively, they could reverse the reforms. When Ghana moved to an auction for foreign exchange in 1986, however, the political conflict ended, because the government restricted its own ability to affect the currency's value. When the government of Jerry Rawlings legalized trading of foreign currencies through privately owned bureaus in 1988, the government gave up its remaining ability to affect the exchange rate and institutionalized a different means for allocating foreign exchange.

Similarly, a one-time increase in agricultural producer prices is not particularly impressive, because prices the next year might not be increased at all. Instead, decontrol of food and agricultural prices—such as has happened in the Central African Republic, Guinea, Madagascar, Mali, Niger, Nigeria, and Uganda[12]—is a much stronger commitment to good agricultural pricing in the long term. Substantively and symbolically, changes in economic institutions are a clear indication that the pro-adjustment forces have consolidated their power and have won outright victories, which can only be rescinded with difficulty. Thus, a focus on reform of basic institutions is a particularly appropriate way for the United States to evaluate commitment to reform.

Concentrating on institutional changes in evaluating African countries may help retain the constituency for aiding Africa in the United States. Such a perspective is more in line with the critique of African economies that AID has developed since 1980: The problems of African economies are structural, and reforming poorly functioning institutions and constructing new policies will take a considerable amount of time. Correspondingly, this perspective indicates that African adjustment and growth will not yield early results, thereby avoiding the problem of dashed expectations. Such a standard could avoid the problem of citing countries that perform well, only to find that those same nations are in utter disarray a few years later.

AID is well positioned to focus on fundamental changes in institutions when evaluating the success of reform efforts. The IMF and World Bank usually have very small missions in African countries. Indeed, the IMF, despite the enormous role it plays in many countries, is unlikely to have more than one or two people in its mission, if it has a mission at all. With such limited personnel, the multilateral organizations have a natural tendency to focus on prices, a measure they can gather easily and analyze quickly with the models they have developed.[13] In addition, it is only natural that organizations composed almost entirely of economists and driven by a powerful economic model would not have a comparative advantage in the analysis of institutional change. The IMF and the World Bank now admit that reforms in the price system have been easier to bring about than other structural changes.[14]

In contrast, AID usually has a much larger mission on the ground and has a close connection with the United States embassy's political section. The AID mission will probably not, however, have a large number of economists. Therefore, focusing on institutional change not only makes sense in evaluating long-term reform, it also plays to AID's comparative bureaucratic advantage. As this chapter makes clear, evaluating the success of reforms in Africa will be a difficult process because significant progress will take time. The following chapters examine some of the specific issues that the United States will have to confront as it implements its reformulated aid policy.

4

THE FUTURE OF AFRICAN ECONOMIES

As the United States continues to promote economic reform in Africa through its bilateral programs and the multilateral institutions, it will confront many difficult issues. In particular, the economic role of the state and the effect of adjustment on the poor are problems of great concern to Africans and will present many difficulties for American diplomacy. Since the resolution of these issues requires going beyond the basic dogma of "getting prices right," the United States will have to be particularly careful and innovative. The United States will no longer be able to follow the lead of the World Bank and the IMF, but will have to develop nuanced policies of its own.

It is important to approach issues related to the design of African economies with humility. Western advice has contributed to many of the policy disasters still afflicting economies across the continent. For example, advisors from developed countries and from the World Bank encouraged Africans to establish some of the state-owned firms that have performed so poorly over the last twenty years. Even if Western advice turns out to be remarkably successful, African economies will only grow slowly, and consumption levels will not change markedly for the foreseeable future. Although the United States should press forcefully for what it believes is best, it must constantly be aware of the limits of its own alternatives and sensitive to factors in each country that call for nuance and redesign of particular policies.

The Economic Role of the State

A central aspect of adjustment in African countries concerns reforming the state apparatus. At the most basic level, many African governments chronically spend more than they earn. In 1987, the latest year for which data are available, the average African country ran a deficit equivalent to 23 percent of expenditures.[1] African states have also enacted a large number of regulations affecting commercial activities that have often hindered entrepreneurs. Because the state often controls access to foreign exchange and the prices of goods, and routine business transactions require official government approval, many regulations encourage corruption.

In addition, most African countries possess highly inefficient state enterprises that consistently lose money and inhibit the private sector from operating. Unfortunately, even by African standards, the data on public sector enterprise performance are sparse and lack consistent definitions. What little systematic analysis there is suggests that African state-owned enterprises have performed extremely poorly. In one study of West African countries, 62 percent of the public enterprises showed net losses while 36 percent had a negative net worth.[2] Other studies indicate that in Benin, Mali, Sudan, Nigeria, Mauritania, Zaire, Sierra Leone, and Senegal, public enterprises have accumulated losses that sometimes amount to a significant percentage of the total economy.[3] The comments of the head of Ghana's State Enterprise Commission would be appropriate for many countries: "Public enterprises . . . have succeeded to combine public sector inefficiency and stagnation with private sector insensitivity to the public interest."[4]

Much of the debate over structural adjustment has concentrated on reforming the role of the African state in the economy. The United States has advocated that states shrink dramatically in Africa, both to reduce public deficits and to eliminate distortionary policies. The issue of privatization has generated considerable controversy. The United States has been particularly bold in pushing its view that future growth must come from a reinvigorated private sector that absorbs functions previously allocated to the state. The President's Task Force on International Private Enterprise wrote in 1984, "We owe it not only to ourselves, but to the people of the developing countries, to try to persuade their governments that what we believe to be true is, in fact, true: that the key to development lies in a vigorous public sector." The task force recognized that such a strong posture would alienate many, but argued that "while pandering may be good politics in the short run, it is bad politics in the long run."[5]

As a result, privatization of state-owned enterprises has been the focus of AID's efforts to help reform the state sector in Africa and other developing countries. In 1986, every AID mission was directed to promote privatization efforts. AID guidelines now clearly state that in order for it to help a state enterprise, it should be moving toward market-based operations and divestiture. In particular, AID funds "should not be used solely to improve the ability of state-owned corporations to respond to market forces."[6] Rather, for the United States to aid publicly owned firms, the government should have the clear intention of privatizing the company as soon as possible.

The U.S. position equates market forces and the private sector. No doubt, this position evolved in good part because of the highly inefficient and unresponsive operations of state enterprises worldwide. In Africa, however, where economies function radically differently from the West, it is especially important that the policies make sense because of conditions on the ground rather than because they work in the United States.

In fact, privatization is not going to significantly change the economic landscape of most African countries in the short or medium term. First, the anti–private sector policies that successive African governments followed for twenty years prior to the early 1980s have meant that very few people have the capital and the management skills to acquire significant public enterprises. For example, in West African countries, many of those that have the capital and skills to take over state firms are Lebanese, who are politically unacceptable to most governments. Similarly, in Kenya (a country with a relatively sophisticated capital market), privatization has been slow because of government concerns that only foreigners or politically unacceptable local citizens (for example, Indians or Kikuyus) could purchase the companies from the state.[7]

In addition, many private firms in Africa are corrupt, continuing to operate solely because of distortionary government policies. Many companies in Africa would not exist if they did not have preferential access to foreign exchange and government contracts, operate behind high tariff walls, or have monopolies in their domestic market. Indeed, before structural adjustment can enhance the private sector, many firms will have to go out of business because they depended on government-induced distortions to survive. Given the trauma that reform inflicts on the private sector, it is unlikely that large-scale privatizations can occur in the immediate future.

Furthermore, it is doubtful that many of the companies that governments most want to sell are viable. The state-owned enterprises that African governments initially singled out for privatization often owe significant sums in back taxes and contributions to unfunded pension schemes, their physical plants are run-down, and many have almost no managerial capacity. Indeed, they are often chosen for privatization not because they would be viable firms in the private sector (as in the UK and other European countries) but because they have already collapsed. In the end, many of these companies will probably have to be shut down and their assets sold for scrap.[8] The rhetoric of privatization and market forces should not be allowed to obscure the reality of state-owned enterprises in Africa: these companies were barely functioning in the state sector, and their privatization will be a torturous affair.

Finally, privatization is exceptionally controversial in Africa because it is seen as compromising the hard-won economic sovereignty that these countries have achieved since independence. For better or worse, state firms in many countries are powerful symbols that the government has seized the commanding heights of the economy from foreigners. Despite the widespread agreement that these firms have operated inefficiently, the possibility of selling what some still view as the nation's patrimony can arouse considerable nationalist sentiment. Emotions are only further aggravated when it is suggested that large parts of the old state sector be sold to foreigners or ethnic minorities.

As a result, enthusiasm for privatization has faded substantially. The World Bank has already made it clear that it believes that privatization is not a viable option for many state firms in Africa. Rather, the World Bank has concentrated on improving the commercial activities of firms that will remain in the state sector so that they can be more responsive to market forces.[9] Indeed, the World Bank has probably spent more money improving enterprises that will remain in the public sector than on its efforts at privatization. All donors have now realized that, by concentrating on privatization, they had chosen a policy that attracted the maximum animus from African governments while delivering the least in terms of producing market-responsive firms.

Thus, there has been a new emphasis on finding creative solutions to make state firms more market-responsive. Reform of the state sector is an especially attractive option because of the weakness of the private sector and because foreign capital, which could play a crucial role in promoting industrialization, currently shows little interest in Africa. In addition, economic theory suggests that there is nothing wrong with state ownership as long as firms are allowed to respond to prices and follow commercial considerations.

Thus, the U.S. regulation prohibiting aid that helps state-owned firms become more efficient seems ill-conceived.

Further, contrary to the initial rhetoric of the United States, African countries need activist states. These states, however, must act in ways that enhance market forces rather than, as in past, obstructing commercial activity. In Ghana, for example, structural adjustment has meant the rehabilitation, reconstruction, and construction of the road, phone, and electrical networks. The World Bank since 1983 has concentrated on road reconstruction as a crucial area, because even the most rudimentary economic activity, such as shipping cocoa to the ports, will not be profitable if the poor condition of the roads causes transport costs to be too high. Despite the fact that the World Bank has devoted a significant amount of money to road construction in Ghana since 1983, it will not be until the late 1990s that the Ghanaian roads will be back to the condition they were at independence in 1957.

Correspondingly, the state can also help strengthen market forces by fostering the development of capital and futures markets. The banking and finance sectors of almost all African countries are extremely weak. Companies must look exclusively to banks for capital. In many countries, however, credit in the banking sector is locked up because of defaults by state-owned enterprises and because of the tremendous changes wrought by structural adjustment. The state will have to intervene if financial sectors are to operate more efficiently in the future.

It is the Western historical experience that a strong and well-funded state is needed for a dynamic private sector. In East Asia, the state in all of the fast growing countries has played a significant role in providing infrastructure and establishing a set of incentives to promote exports and sectoral development. In fact, in all but Hong Kong, East Asian intervention went far beyond what the neoclassical formulas usually suggest as desirable. For example, in South Korea,

"Hyundai was nominated as sole maker of marine engines, Kia was ordered to cease car making, and Daewoo marine-engine manufacturing; fifty-three of the sixty-eight shipping companies were collapsed into sixteen."[10] Similarly, in Taiwan, "the government remains dominant in such fields as heavy machinery, steel, aluminum, shipbuilding, petroleum, synthetics, fertilizers, engineering, and recently, semiconductors. Almost every bank in Taiwan is also wholly or partially owned by the state. . . . "[11]

Most of East Asian state intervention, however, was done in a manner that eventually promoted the private sector and exports in particular. In contrast, in Africa state intervention has often led to the strangulation of the private sector and gross inefficiency.[12] The question is not the degree of state intervention; rather, the issue is whether the manner of state intervention promotes growth or retards it. This perspective is unfortunately missed by those proponents who argue simply that the private sector should supply most of Africa's future growth.

The analysis developed above suggests that the size of the state is not an interesting consideration by itself. What is important is that the state perform the roles that it can do best and withdraw from areas where the analysis suggests it is doing too much damage. If the state is larger after this redistribution, it should not matter. In fact, evidence suggests that in many African countries, the state will actually have to expand to fulfill the tasks it must accomplish if the economy is to grow. Just the extraordinary expenses that will have to be incurred to (re)construct the infrastructure will require significant state expansion.

The next decade of reform of the African state apparatus will therefore have to be much more nuanced than the advice given in the 1980s. Instead of using a chainsaw to cut off the limbs of the state, a scalpel must be applied to divest the state of the functions it is performing poorly while strengthening the overall apparatus. While the World Bank will play the lead role in the new effort to reform the state, it does not necessarily have the analytic talents and field experience to advise African countries on these difficult reforms. Thus, the United States can play an especially important role in helping African countries reorient their states to promote growth in the most effective manner possible.

There are several potential areas the United States might concentrate on to help African states restructure themselves. First, many African administrative structures fell into disrepair during the long economic decline and need to be rehabilitated. Staff need to be trained, organizations provided with basic technical information, and, in some cases, buildings repaired before African states can function properly and foster economic growth. Second, African states need to decentralize some of their economic decision-making to the local level. One of the main reasons for the urban bias in many African countries is the concentration of almost all decision-making authority in the capital. Third, African states must establish impermeable barriers between politicians and state enterprises that will continue to be owned by the state. If politics impinges less on state-owned enterprises, they may be able to operate in a manner similar to commercial firms. AID is already working in several of these areas but must expand its scope if revitalized African states are to contribute to economic growth. Indeed, given that many of these reforms require institutional expertise but do not cost significant amounts, AID may be in a particularly good position to reorient the economic role of the African state.

Economic Reform and the Poor

By its very nature, economic reform involves large transfers of income. Policies such as devaluation and raising the prices paid to farmers seek to fundamentally alter who wins and who loses in African economies. Not surprisingly, there has been considerable concern expressed over the fate of those who might lose out during reform, even if overall economies benefit. In their major UNICEF document, *Adjustment with a Human Face*, Giovanni Andrea Cornia, Richard Jolley, and Frances Stewart argue that the costs placed on the poor in structural adjustment programs are just too great, because decreases in government subsidies, drastic cuts in social programs, and implementation of disinflationary macroeconomic programs pose life-threatening dangers to women, children, and the aged. Instead, they argue that it is time to move away from conventional approaches to adjustment and toward an adjustment process that focuses clearly on the needs of the poorest groups.[13] The UNICEF report initiated an emotional debate over how the programs recommended by Western donors are affecting the poor in Africa and other parts of the developing world.

The effect of adjustment on the poor is a contentious issue that will continue to confront Western efforts to promote economic reform. Many in Africa, of course, are concerned about the effect of the reform programs on the poor. There are, however, many others who have simply latched onto the poverty issue in order to oppose the entire thrust of reform effort. For the opponents of economic reform, the poverty issue is an especially good one because it further aggravates African sensibilities already disturbed by the large amount of Western interference in their economies. Also, Western governments and the multilateral institutions have been reluctant to defend their programs against charges of hurting the poor, partially because they too feel uneasy about their role in the African reform process.

As a result, efforts to help and protect the poorest are increasingly part of economic reform programs. As noted previously, Congress is trying to force AID to devote resources to poverty amelioration. In addition, many existing structural adjustment programs have added new components that try to protect the fortunes of the poorest during economic reform. *The Economist* has gone so far as to suggest that the efforts to help the poor are causing a revival in all but name of the basic needs philosophy of the 1970s.[14] As efforts to help the poor increasingly influence the structure of reform programs, it is particularly important to examine the issue.

One of the clearest arguments for focusing on the fate of the poor during adjustment is a simple moral claim that this is the right thing to do. This argument is actually quite complicated. The issue often forgotten in debates about how adjustment affects the poor is that almost everyone in sub-Saharan Africa is absolutely poor by almost any conceivable measure. The average per capita income in Africa is $340 and life expectancy is 51 years at birth.[15] In a continent where almost everyone is poor, the Western notion that the poorest have a particular claim may not be as strong as it is in developed societies.

In particular, the cost of reaching the poorest in terms of forgone opportunities for the large number of other poor people in African countries must be assessed. If reaching the poorest 5 to 10 percent of the population costs more than helping a much larger number of routinely poor people, the moral claim becomes especially problematic.

Also, concentrating on the poor causes people to miss the fact that Africans are impoverished not because of distribution problems but because their economies as a whole do not produce enough. As Dr. Joseph Abbey, one of the architects of Ghana's reform program, noted,

> People who live in rich countries see poverty as pathological which can be solved through policies. Those who object to people living in cardboard houses in rich countries come to Africa and think that they are seeing the same thing when they see people living in cardboard. This tends to put problems of redistribution at the center of political debate rather than questions of production.[16]

A focus on redistribution is especially inappropriate in Africa where economies must, on average, grow by 3.1 percent each year just to stay even with population growth. Many economies will have to grow by a significant amount just to get back to where they were at independence in the 1960s.

This is not to say that all of the efforts to restructure social spending during adjustment is misguided. Some programs have proven their worth over the long term. For example, it is absolutely vital that African countries continue to invest in human capital through education at all times. Rather, the relevant policy question is: How much should concerns for alleviating poverty enter into decisions about the design of structural adjustment programs?

It is important to understand who the poor are and what they do. While data on socioeconomic conditions in Africa is sparse, recent research makes one conclusion very clear: The poor live in the rural areas. In Ghana, one study found that 80 percent of the poor and almost all of the poorest are in the rural areas outside of Accra.[17] Similarly, in a survey of Côte d'Ivoire, researchers found that while 59 percent of all Ivorians live in the rural areas, 86 percent of the poorest 30 percent of the population and 96 percent of the poorest 10 percent of the population live outside the cities.[18] The fact that the poor live largely in the rural areas, far from the capital, is particularly important when evaluating the effect of structural adjustment programs. Because of their administrative and fiscal weaknesses, African governments have very little institutionalized presence in the rural areas, so it is unlikely that most government programs help the truly poor. Correspondingly, if government programs are cut during structural adjustment, the poorest will not be significantly affected. In the Côte d'Ivoire study, it was found that establishing user fees for medical care would not affect the truly poor because they seldom had access to a doctor or a nurse for their ailments.[19] Similarly, decreases in public sector employment will not affect the truly poor because they are seldom, if ever, employed by government. The Côte d'Ivoire study found that if all the heads of poor households who worked for government were to lose their jobs, only 2 percent of the poorest 30 percent of the population and only 1 percent of the poorest 10 percent would be affected.[20]

Similarly, cuts in government subsidies, usually demanded by the IMF and the World Bank in order to reduce the fiscal deficit, are seen as measures which hurt the poor. In many African countries, however, subsidies are used to buy the political support of the relatively affluent rather than to relieve poverty. For example, in Côte d'Ivoire, rental subsidies help the rich, not the poor. Similarly, the poor do not receive a significant percentage of other amenities such as access to drinking water.[21]

The isolation of the African poor from government programs is an important point missed by many in the West who believe that, as in their own countries, cuts in government social programs and government employment will inevitably hurt the poorest. Rather, reform programs are most likely to disadvantage poorer segments of urban society who gained access to limited government social programs and employment due to their location. While the urban poor in African countries are impoverished by any measure, they are not the poorest in their own countries.

Given the administrative weaknesses of African governments, it is much more likely that the poor will be affected by changes in prices than cuts in or expansion of government programs. Adjustment programs have the potential to actually help the poor. In particular, higher prices for farmers and improved agrarian services—the very heart of most orthodox economic programs—are far better poverty alleviation measures than government-provided social services in the vast majority of African countries. Advantageous prices are the very opposite of "trickle down" policies because they encourage the poor to expand their participation in the production process for their own benefit. It should be noted that the poorest in African countries are probably not producing crops that would be affected by the national market in the short term. Indeed, poor pricing policies may have forced them to retreat to near-subsistence production. Over the long term, however, better prices for farmers may encourage at least some of the poor to enter the market again, to their benefit.

It is also important to recognize that eliminating distortions in an economy can have a beneficial impact on the poor. For example, when goods are distributed on the black market because of distortionary government policies, the poor probably pay above the market clearing price.[22] The black market price includes a risk premium and a rent component derived by those with privileged access to goods. Liberalization of price controls may actually ease poor people's access to goods, a fact obscured by official inflation figures that primarily examine controlled prices.[23]

Precisely because they are poor and far from markets, however, the poorest may not have even been affected by these distortions and will not benefit if adjustment programs "get the prices right." Therefore, the most likely result, due to their economic and geographic condition, is that the poor will not be affected significantly by any adjustment program in the short run. In the long run, there is some reason to believe that they could benefit because the terms of trade will be changed in their favor.

Correspondingly, government programs that seek to help the poor probably will not accomplish a great deal. For instance, Ghana, through its Programme to Ameliorate the Social Costs of Adjustment (PAMSCAD) has tried to reduce the effect of adjustment on the poor by creating a large number of public employment programs and helping laid-off civil servants to get new jobs in agriculture. Precisely because of the poor's location, however, PAMSCAD has been bedeviled by a huge number of administrative problems since it was first proposed in 1988. A program such as PAMSCAD, which requires literally hundreds of administrative systems in the rural areas, is precisely the kind of program that an African government finds most difficult to implement.

Indeed, because of Ghana's administrative problems in reaching the poorest, the PAMSCAD money that was supposed to go to the impoverished has been redirected to areas where the state already has a relatively strong administrative apparatus; that is, precisely the areas that have traditionally benefited from government programs. In contrast, putting money directly in the hands of the rural poor by making the economic activities they engage in more rewarding will do far more for them than government programs, which are usually highly unorganized at the rural level.

More generally, ad hoc poverty alleviation programs sponsored by aid donors and governments are simply no substitute for long-term economic growth, which allows for the natural establishment of social services in a more lasting manner. For example, the conventional wisdom is that Kenya has adopted a long-term policy of economic growth at the expense of social services while Tanzania, though sacrificing some prosperity, has been far more successful in devoting resources to social welfare programs. An examination of the actual statistics, however, suggests that because Kenya's overall economic policies promoted economic growth and a relatively prosperous government financial base over a long period of time, it not only has a much higher Gross National Product per capita than Tanzania (US$370 versus US$110 in 1990) but it also has developed a better social service base. Life expectancy at birth is 59 years in Kenya compared to 48 years in Tanzania, while in 1989 94 percent of all Kenyan children were in primary schools, compared to 63 percent for Tanzania. Only approximately 4 percent of all eligible children in Tanzania attend secondary school as opposed to 23 percent in Kenya.[24] Tanzania's economic policies were so poor that the government could not finance its social goals.

Thus, those who picture the World Bank and AID as choosing macroeconomic reform over health clinics and other readily available programs for the poor are painting a false dichotomy. Unless countries stabilize their economies and adopt programs that will promote growth, the clinics that will be built will soon have no medicine, the schools will have no books, and the nascent environmental programs will fade into disrepair.

The United States must be much clearer on the question of the poor during structural adjustment. Poor people in Africa cannot be helped by redistributive government programs alone. The poorest often cannot be reached by these programs and African governments do not have the administrative systems or the fiscal base to sustain them. Therefore, blanket programs aimed at the poor to alleviate presumedly harmful effects of structural adjustment should be viewed with suspicion. On the other hand, specific interventions in education or health that take account of the existing administrative infrastructure may be of enormous benefit.

To alleviate poverty in African countries, it is vital that policies be devised to increase overall production. The United States, as the clearest international advocate of economic reform, has an especially important role in making sure that adjustment programs stay focused on increasing production. The World Bank is often justified in complaining that it is advocating policies that the United States and other Western countries support, but that it finds few allies when the highly charged issue of economic reforms' effect on the poor is raised. AID must make it clear that, in the end, the most compassionate policies are those that promote overall economic growth.

5

THE AFRICAN DEBT PROBLEM

A critical barrier to economic reform in Africa is the debt problem. If the United States and other donors are going to help African countries reform, the debt crisis must be addressed. By 1991, total sub-Saharan Africa debt stock was projected to be $176 billion, a 214 percent increase over the 1980 level. Even more importantly, debt service obligations are extremely high. In 1991, approximately 21 percent of the total value of African exports had to be committed to debt service.[1] In countries that already face dramatic shortages of imports necessary for industry and agriculture, this level of debt service is an extreme burden. In fact, only twelve African countries have serviced their debt continuously since 1980.[2] As Reginald Green notes, current African debt levels are "objectively unmanageable with existing terms, conditions, and export prospects."[3]

The debt problem explains why, despite the large amounts of money that Western countries have committed to African economic reform, capital inflows to the continent are only slightly greater than capital outflows.[4] Indeed, net transfers from the IMF during the last half of the 1980s were consistently negative.[5] These extremely low levels of net transfers are simply unacceptable if African countries are to develop. Structural adjustment of the type recommended by the World Bank and the United States is predicated on large new flows of finance to African countries because, even under the most optimistic scenarios, economic reform by itself cannot solve the African debt problem.[6]

In addition to being a drag on development, the large overhang of debt in African countries has a particularly pernicious psychological effect. Debt can be seen as a tax on successful reformers: the better a country begins to perform due to domestic policy changes, the greater its outflow of capital to meet old debts and new ones that it incurred early in the adjustment process. The debt tax on adjustment produces an environment where African leaders come to believe that their countries can never grow again, no matter what they do. This debt tax on adjusters is particularly worrisome given the need to create demonstrative successes in Africa.

Two aspects of African debt are important to note in designing a viable solution to the problem. First, African debt is relatively small by world standards, amounting to only 14 percent of total developing country debt.[7] Further, 21 percent of total African debt is accounted for by Nigeria, which because of its size and the characteristics of its debt is usually treated as a special case.[8] Second, most African debt, unlike the debt of Latin American countries, is owed to official creditors, either other governments or multilateral organizations such as the IMF and the World Bank. In 1991, official creditors and multilateral organizations were projected to account for approximately 74 percent of total African debt while private creditors accounted for only 26 percent of the debt. In contrast, 35 percent of Latin American debt is owed to official creditors.[9] African debt is therefore potentially more tractable because it can be systematically reduced by direct government action.

Some progress has been made on at least the public debt that African countries owe individual Western governments. The Toronto Agreement, finalized in Berlin in 1988, gave Western countries a variety of options to choose from to reduce the effective debt of low income countries in sub-Saharan Africa. Accordingly, the United States adopted a program to relieve the debt burden of African countries. Of the $4.5 billion sub-Saharan countries owe to the United States, approximately $1 billion is in development loans that the United States is now willing to cancel. For a country to be eligible for debt relief, it must demonstrate its intention to reform its economy by signing an agreement with the IMF or the World Bank.[10]

The Toronto menu approach, however, will not significantly reduce the overall African debt problem. For example, if the Toronto terms are repeatedly applied and no other debt relief is offered, by the year 2000, nonconcessional debt will have been reduced by only 11 percent.[11] A good part of the problem is the debt owed to the multilateral institutions, which is not covered by the Toronto agreement. In 1989, debt payments to the IMF and the World Bank accounted for 50.2 percent of total African debt servicing, compared to 17.6 percent for bilateral debt and 32.1 for private credits.[12] In fact, some countries are now unable to service their debts even to the multilaterals.

Yet little progress has been made in trying to resolve the debt owed by African countries to the multilaterals. There are, in fact, some very good reasons for the multilaterals to be hesitant about granting debt relief. Much of their own credibility with international financial markets and developed countries rests on the obligation debtors feel to pay back the multilaterals first. Although Africa's debt is small by the standards of both the IMF and the World Bank, both organizations are concerned that debt relief could set an extremely bad precedent. The multilateral institutions also face legal barriers to offering debt relief, given how their funding legislation is written.

This concern may not be as significant as the multilaterals believe. Both the World Bank and the IMF have been under pressure from the United States and other bilateral donors to make significant concessions to African countries for a decade. In particular, new facilities with greater funding have been established that are not available to other countries. The large debt-distressed countries (for example, Brazil and Argentina), the ones that really could put stress on IMF and World Bank financing, have not given any evidence of resenting Africa's special treatment. Indeed, they seem to want to differentiate themselves from African economies—widely perceived as basketcases—because nations such as Brazil and Argentina still seek to attract significant private finance and foreign investment. The World Bank itself is now increasingly explicit in differentiating African economies from others in the developing world.[13] Given how peculiarly weak African countries are, multilateral debt relief may not establish a strong precedent.

There has also been little movement on multilateral debt because there is no institutional imperative for either the IMF or the World Bank to consider the debt problem when proposing economic reforms for African countries. The IMF is primarily interested in seeing that African countries resolve balance of payments problems and therefore concentrates on proposals that reduce internal demand and that can be implemented in two to three years. Similarly, the World Bank has been involved mainly in lending for specific projects and has only recently been willing to lend money to fund structural reforms of African economies. There is, therefore, no direct link between the reforms actually carried out by African countries and the multilateral debt that they owe. As a result, even if African countries fully embrace the economic reforms suggested by outside authorities, debt problems could still overwhelm them and destroy hope for future growth.

In the end, it must be recognized that a substantial portion of African debt, especially that owed by the poorest countries, is not going to be collected. The question is not whether there should be debt relief. Rather, the question is whether debt relief will be issued in a manner that promotes economic reform or in an ad hoc manner too late to help most countries. Indeed, the IMF has now recognized that some African countries are not going to pay their debt and has launched an intricate program to allow these countries to borrow more even though they are technically in default. These ad hoc programs, however, do not address the structural inability of many African countries to pay their debt. While the multilaterals may, through a series of increasingly generous ad hoc debt relief programs, eventually address the debt problem, they will have wasted a great deal of time and stunted the growth of many African countries for years to come.

The multilaterals should immediately begin to look to ways to relieve African debt as long as forgiveness is linked to progress on economic reforms. Indeed, the link should be even more demanding than the current conditionality clauses in IMF and World Bank loans. If creditors do not demand further reform as the price for debt relief, African leaders may feel less pressure to continue to adjust their economies. Clearly, the worst possible result of debt relief would be if a decrease in external obligations allowed African leaders to revert to the old economic practices that brought their countries to ruin. The linkage between debt and economic reform can be strengthened by relieving debt in small tranches each time a country meets an agreed-upon milepost.

The debt reduction can be done in creative ways to promote further development. For example, the individual country debt can be transformed into local currency obligations which are paid into a fund to improve infrastructure and rehabilitate the private sector. Undoubtedly, other innovative mechanisms can tie debt relief to further economic reform.

A clear role for the United States is to provide the political leadership within the multilaterals to address the debt problem. As the most important donor in both organizations, the United States will have to support any multilateral debt reduction policy for it to succeed. Particular U.S. support will be needed given the legal and political obstacles. This will not be an easy step for the United States. Congressional support for the multilaterals is limited, and debt reduction by the IMF and the World Bank, after they had specifically promised to collect all their debts, may raise considerable congressional ire. Congress and the public will have to be convinced that the money owed is not going to be collected regardless, and that African reform will not occur without debt reduction by the multilaterals.

Unfortunately, the structure of the U.S. government makes a constructive policy toward multilateral debt particularly difficult. The State Department and AID are the lead agencies in promoting economic reform in African countries and have the clearest vision of how the debt overhang is short-circuiting reform efforts. U.S. policy toward the multilaterals, however, is made by the Treasury, which is naturally reluctant to endorse any policy which forgoes revenue. Thus, any comprehensive policy toward promoting economic reform in Africa must convince Treasury that a narrow focus on African countries meeting their debt obligations may force these countries to view the very process of economic reform as futile.

This focus on multilateral debt does not mean that more could not be done to forgive existing bilateral debt, as noted in the analysis of the Toronto terms. In particular, the United States should explore more generous debt forgiveness measures that provide benefits to low- and middle-income African countries. Following from the analysis developed in this chapter, any additional debt forgiveness must be tied to even more substantial reforms by African countries. Thus, there should be no general debt relief but further consideration given on a case-by-case basis.

The United States and other developed countries spent much of the 1980s trying to convince African countries that reform was in their best interests. Now, substantial, but uneven, enthusiasm exists across the continent for structural reform. In the 1990s, the United States and other donors must move beyond rhetoric to look at the basic international constraints, especially debt, affecting African countries. If the debt problem is not addressed soon, the efforts of the

1980s, including the billions of dollars of aid committed by Western countries, will have been wasted. Indeed, a fair program of debt relief would be an important sign to Africa that the United States and other developed countries are intent on reforming international economic structures as long as African countries engage in earnest reform.

6

ECONOMIC REFORM AND POLITICAL LIBERALIZATION

With the revolutions in Eastern Europe and the wave of democratization that has swept other parts of the third world, especially Latin America, new attention has been focused on the relationship between economic reform and political liberalization in Africa. Indeed, there are now pressures inside the U.S. government, especially in Congress, to tie aid not only to changes in economic policy but also to political reforms such as multiparty elections. The issue of whether and how U.S. aid should be used to pursue political changes will be one of the most important challenges of the 1990s.

Some aspects of American policy are already clear. First, the question of aiding severe human rights abusers, a critical issue during the Cold War, has for the most part already been resolved. Congress has made it clear that it will block U.S. aid to countries where torture and imprisonment without trial are common. The executive branch will probably be much more hesitant about even raising the question of aid to human rights abusers, because the strategic imperative to help these regimes has vanished. Rather, the question for the United States is how much it should be actively involved in helping African countries engage in political reform to break with the authoritarian, personalistic governments that have been so common across the continent.

The relationship between economic and political changes is one of the great questions of social science; unfortunately, it is particularly susceptible to simplistic analysis and wishful thinking. For years it was thought that Third World countries faced a cruel choice between well-performing economies with authoritarian governments, or suffering economies with governments that granted more civil liberties, but could not make tough, unpopular decisions. The poor performance, however, of the old Eastern European regimes and the democratization of Latin America during economic depression swept that idea aside.

There are currently two partially distinct arguments about the relationship between political and economic reform that have to be analyzed. The first argues that some political reform is necessary for proposed economic reforms to be sustained. For example, in the World Bank's recent report on Africa, it suggested that peasants and other groups had to possess a degree of countervailing power so that pro-rural sector policies could continue.[1] This perspective clearly seeks to continue focusing on economic reforms but acknowledges that there must be changes in the political system because so many of the unsound policies adopted in Africa had political origins. In addition, economic reforms in African countries must develop domestic political support if bilateral and multilateral donors are to take a less intrusive posture in the future.

Ideally, growth and the changed economic environment will cause many African countries to develop new constituencies for adjustment naturally. For example, significant increases in agricultural production and the new awareness of how directly agriculture affects African economies may make leaders think twice in the future about policies that tax farmers through low producer prices. Similarly, properly valued exchange rates may create new exporters who can exert significant pressure to prevent a recurrence of the old policy of overvalued exchange rates.

Political constituencies, however, may not form overnight to support new policies, so continued donor pressure will be appropriate. In Africa, the rural population, one of the chief beneficiaries of structural adjustment, is atomistically dispersed across the countryside and faces severe logistical problems in trying to coalesce into a significant interest group. Indeed, the urban population will always retain a significant amount of power by virtue of their ability to riot. Therefore, groups supporting economic reform may not become politically powerful for a long period of time. Inevitably, some of the early beneficiaries of reform will be foreign investors, citizens with a foreign background (for example, Indians and Lebanese), or members of minority ethnic groups who are politically suspect and who cannot actively pressure the government.

The United States and other international donors should promote with a very light hand political reforms that sustain economic adjustment. Rather than directly intervene in the national political arena (for example, the issue of multiparty elections), the United States and other donors can concentrate on helping African countries redesign institutions so that a repetition of poor economic policies is less likely. For example, a number of African countries have gone beyond raising prices paid to farmers; they abolished their agricultural marketing boards so that the state has much less of an effect on farmers' incomes and it is much harder for the urban population to bring pressure to bear on pricing decisions. By devolving pricing decisions to the market, these reforms emasculated the urban population because they could no longer use their old tactics, especially riots directed at the government, to influence the price of food. Correspondingly, this type of reform amounts to an empowerment of the rural population, because the government is no longer able to control their incomes directly.

Similarly, U.S. pressure could be brought to bear for African countries not only to devalue but to devolve control of their exchange rate mechanism to the market. A host of other political reforms that support economic adjustment are also possible. For example, the establishment of property rights, and the corresponding strengthening of the judiciary, is a clear requirement for large-scale new investment from either domestic or foreign sources. Indeed, many foreign and African investors report that one of the major obstacles to business is that contracts can rarely be enforced. As a result, government actions are more likely to be conducted on an ad hoc basis according to the preferences of individual officials rather than an acknowledged body of regulations and laws. African countries must establish better legal systems if they expect the tough economic reforms they are enacting to produce a supply response.

Reforms that institutionalize economic liberalization would also move toward political liberalization because they would significantly reduce the scope of the overbearing African state. With considerably more latitude in the economic sphere, African citizens could establish, over time, important bases of power independent of the state. Since these reforms would be linked directly to economic reform, they would be less likely to be viewed as uncontrolled Western interference in the affairs of African countries. Also, political reforms tied directly to adjustment would fit comfortably into the outlines of a reformulated aid policy described previously because economic growth would still be the highest priority.

Aid Should Not Be Conditioned on Political Reform

The second, still emerging, perspective focuses primarily on the desirability of political liberalization and sees economic reform and growth as springing naturally from desirable changes in the political system. For example, President Bush said when he addressed the joint meeting of the World Bank and the IMF in 1989, "In the end, both economic freedom and political freedom are essential and inseparable companions on the road to national prosperity."[2] While proposals are still being formulated, some who hold this grander vision of economic reform and political liberalization believe that U.S. aid should now also be used to directly promote political liberalization and, especially, elections. This view has obviously become more popular given the excitement caused by the revolutions in Eastern Europe.

This perspective has a number of problems that must be examined in detail. First, America's cognitive limits in promoting political change should be clear. Bilateral and multilateral donors were confident in recommending stabilization and structural adjustment programs because they had a powerful theory—based on neoclassical microeconomics—that offered both a critique of African economics and possible solutions. Even with this well developed theory, adjustment programs often fail for a myriad of reasons. There is no similar theory to promote wholesale political liberalization. Indeed, the fact that previous theorizing on the relationship between economic and political change was so wrong should disabuse everyone of the idea that there are easy solutions or automatic laws that the United States can follow to promote global political reform.

In fact, the relationship between overall economic growth and political freedom is quite complicated. Many of the best economic performers in the Third World over the last twenty years, especially the East Asian tigers, could not be considered politically liberal. In addition, the second echelon newly industrializing countries—including Thailand, Indonesia, Malaysia—are by and large not democratic. These countries, however, have developed political structures which undergird economic policies that promote growth.

Further, it would be inappropriate to tie aid to political reform solely on the basis of the recent, dramatic events, which have seen significant political openings in roughly half of all African countries. The wave of political reform sweeping across Africa makes it tempting to believe that politics in Africa has changed so fundamentally that a reversion by many countries to military or authoritarian rule is unthinkable, especially when the rest of the world is also moving, almost uniformly, to greater political liberalization. It is sobering to remember that between 1954 and 1961, Latin

America experienced military disengagement from politics in eleven countries and some claimed that politics had changed forever. In the mid-1960s, however, a "tidal wave" of coups took place across that continent.[3] Claude Welch's warning that military withdrawal from politics cannot be considered successful until soldiers have been in their barracks for ten years and there has been one successful transition should serve as a further warning that the current euphoria should not be allowed to cloud analytic judgments.[4]

The history of democratization elsewhere in the world should serve as a warning that many of the current attempts at political liberalization in African countries will fail. Democratization in Europe took hundreds of years and, while the world has learned a great deal about the workings of political systems (for example, the consequences of electoral laws such as proportional representation), there is little reason to believe that political liberalization can be accomplished in a short period of time. Indeed, as Andre Lijphart has consistently pointed out, even European democracies vary widely. For example, the United Kingdom has a highly centralized political system that encourages a small number of parties to compete for power and does not have a written constitution. In contrast, Switzerland has a decentralized system of power with a proportional representation system that encourages many parties to operate according to a highly detailed constitution.[5] These highly nuanced political systems developed in response to the particular political and social conditions existing in the respective countries. They evolved over decades, at least in partially in response to political failures.

African countries, if they are to be successful in political liberalization, will need equally nuanced political systems, each designed to cope with a unique constellation of political and social forces. Such complex political arrangements cannot be created overnight and will probably only evolve in response to failure. Indeed, even Indian democracy, one of the notable successes in the Third World over the last forty years, may not yet have developed a set of institutions capable of withstanding the stresses of cultural pluralism.[6] Therefore, many of the current political liberalization efforts in Africa may fail, although this does not mean that African politics will automatically revert to the old, authoritarian patterns. Indeed, there may be even greater scope for the kind of institutional improvements (for example, strengthening of property rights) in political systems that are in flux.

Attempts at political liberalization may also ignite political processes that threaten the very integrity of the nation and that will doom reform, at least in the short run. In Africa, questioning domestic political arrangements may reignite debates about the desirability of the nation itself. The first issue that emerges when politics is liberalized is what the outlines of the political community should be.

In fact, many groups may emerge in a more liberal political environment to demand that they be allowed to leave the existing nation, join another, or create their own political institutions. Already, in Central Europe and the former Soviet Union, political liberalization has reopened old ethnic conflicts, and, as a result, some nations have dissolved. There is no reason to believe that African citizens have a stronger commitment to their nations than people in the Soviet Union, Yugoslavia, or Czechoslovakia. The potential for political liberalization leading to ethnic divisiveness and wholesale boundary change is especially great given that many on the continent perceive the colonially-imposed borders as nonsensical. If boundaries do come under stress, the question of political liberalization in those countries will become moot.

Thus, it is not at all certain what we are currently observing. In five years, it may be clear that many of the upheavals occurring across Africa were the precursors of more open, viable political systems. It is far more likely that in a few years the current experiments in political openness will be seen as the beginning of an extraordinarily complex process from which emerged a few clear successes, some disasters, and many countries only beginning the struggle to design political systems that are appropriate for their own countries. It is not possible to predict which countries will fall into each category.

Even in countries that are succcessful in establishing democracies, it would be a significant mistake to reduce the tie between aid and economic reform. The new democracies of Africa will still be faced with the same problems of fundamentally reforming their economies. Indeed, to give large amounts of money to a government simply because it was elected and thereby inadvertently suggest to the new leadership that economic reform is no longer a pressing issue would be an enormous error. Potentially the greatest threat to the new democracies that do emerge in Africa is the dire condition of their economies. Thus, although the new governments are a vast improvement on the autocrats they replace, the United States and other donors must demand that Africa's new leaders professing democracy implement economic reform to receive aid.

Finally, there is a clear contradiction between the desire to do even more with economic aid and the diminishing resources that the United States has devoted to Africa. The United States has had considerable difficulty developing enough leverage to promote economic reforms. It is doubtful if the same aid resources could do double duty in promoting political reform. Indeed, it has been a common assumption in American aid policy over the last few decades that all good things come together. Unfortunately, actual aid policy has seldom been the beneficiary of such coincidental forces.[7]

This is not to say that the United States should not promote widespread political liberalization in Africa. It should, but must be careful of the policy instruments it uses. Aid money has already been committed to promoting economic reform. To add political conditionality would further dilute United States influence. Furthermore, the tie between economic aid and promoting economic performance has been clearly proven. Indeed, structural adjustment came about in part because donors saw that their projects were failing due to distortions in the macroeconomy.

Nor should this argument be read to suggest that economic reform should come before political reform in African countries. The sequencing of reforms is clearly a decision to be made by African citizens themselves. Indeed, the decisions made domestically will be the most consequential affecting the entire reform process. To the extent that donors have a role, however, they can set clear priorities as to what they can do; they should be equally clear as to where their comparative advantages do not lie.

7

CONCLUSION

The Persian Gulf War dramatically illustrated the widening gap between First World and even reasonably good Third World technology. The semiconductor and software revolution is causing a similar differentiation in almost every other sector of the world economy. If Africa does not begin to grow quickly now, it faces the prospect of never being able to catch up with the dynamic economies of the West and increasing parts of the Third World. In addition, if Africa continues to stagnate, there is probably no chance for political reform, environmental improvement, decreased poverty, and all of the other goals that everyone hopes for Africa. All who are involved in the African effort to reform economic and political structures must therefore be clear as to what is at stake.

With the end of the Cold War, the United States is now in a position to tailor an aid policy toward Africa to the central goal of promoting economic reform. The United States, with its prominent role in the multilaterals (in contrast to the Nordic countries) and its significant presence on the ground in Africa (as opposed to Japan), is especially well qualified to address the increasingly difficult political problems that structural adjustment will encounter in the 1990s. The dramatic increase in aid to Africa, in the midst of the excitement over the revolutions in Central Europe, simply reinforces America's prominence.

The realities of economic reform, however, will try America's patience. The truth is that most policies, most of the time, will not work in Africa. There are too many problems with governments (corruption, poor quality civil services), the international economy (low commodity prices, debt), and the private sector (corruption, firms based on distorted policies) to expect any set of suggested policies to work consistently well. Not surprisingly, after almost a decade of extremely difficult reform, African countries are only now beginning to see the results of their efforts. Certainly, both African governments and Western donors now expect structural adjustment to take decades rather than the three to five years most projected in the early 1980s.

Given that failure will be common, inevitably other issues (for example, political liberalization) will come into fashion and other regions (for example, Central Europe) will suddenly look more promising. There can be, however, no quick fix for Africa. The United States must either husband its limited resources and use them effectively or constantly risk circumventing its own efforts. The great challenge for American policymakers will be to reduce expectations about what reform programs can produce in the short term but convince constituencies in the United States and African governments that the future is still attractive.

While American foreign aid policy is being debated, vast forces for change are sweeping across the African continent. Now, as never before in the independent history of dozens of countries across the continent, fundamental questions are being asked about the basic design of political and economic institutions. Countries such as Angola, Congo, Ethiopia, and Mozambique have disavowed Marxism; countries such as Ghana and Guinea that were once hostile to the West now vigorously encourage foreign investment; and a leader such as Kenneth Kaunda, once a staunch defender of the one-party state, allowed multiparty elections and left office when he lost. What was unimaginable in 1988 had, by 1992, become commonplace.

Indeed, what can be called the postcolonial period is ending in Africa. Symbolically, when Namibia gained its independence in 1990, Africans completed their historic project of liberating the continent from colonialism. The path is now open for Africa to develop a more constructive relationship with the West. The potential for a greater emphasis on development in the relations between rich countries and Africa has also been enhanced by the collapse of socialism as a rival ideology. Finally, Africans now widely agree that many of the economic policies adopted following independence were flawed even if there is not as much enthusiasm for the pro-market reforms as there is in the West. In many African countries there is an acknowledgment, especially in light of the achievement of the East Asian countries, that the continent is being left behind. Many Africans are aware that, given the constant advances in computing and information technologies, if Africa does not begin to grow now, it may never catch up. Therefore, finally, it may be possible for the United States and Africa to develop a partnership that will promote reform and one day lead to a brighter African future.

NOTES

Introduction

1. The World Bank, *World Development Report 1992* (Washington, D.C.: The World Bank, 1992), pp. 221, 269.
2. This total includes $14.1 billion from the IMF to thirty-six sub-Saharan African countries, $6.8 billion from the World Bank, and approximately $6 billion from other donors. Jerry Wolgin, "Fresh Start in Africa: A.I.D. and Structural Adjustment in Africa" (Washington, D.C., mimeo, August 1990), p. 6.
3. See Michael Clough, *Free at Last?* (New York: Council on Foreign Relations, 1992), p. 1.

Chapter 1

1. "Memorandum from the Assistant Secretary of State for Near Eastern, South Asian, and African Affairs (Allen) to the Secretary of State," August 12, 1955, reprinted in John P. Glennon, ed., *Foreign Relations of the United States, 1955-1957: Africa*, vol. XVIII (Washington, D.C.: U.S. Government Printing Office, 1989), pp. 12–17.
2. Policy Planning Council, *Selected Aspects of U.S. Economic Aid Policy for Africa*, July 1961, reprinted in George C. Herring, ed., *The John F. Kennedy National Security Files: Africa: 1961–1963*, microfilm, p. 34.
3. William I. Jones, "The Search for an Aid Policy," in Helen Kitchen, ed., *Africa: From Mystery to Maze* (Lexington, MA: Lexington Books, 1976), p. 348.
4. *Action Program to Implement the Recommendations of the Review by Ambassador Korry of Development Policies and Programs in Africa*, 1966, reprinted in George C. Herring, ed., *The Lyndon B. Johnson National Security Files: Africa: 1963–1969*, microfilm, p. 25.
5. Quoted in Jones, "Search for an Aid Policy," p. 349.
6. Policy Planning Council, *Selected Aspects of U.S. Aid*, pp. 39–40.
7. David D. Newsom, "U.S. and Africa in the Post–Cold War Era," *The Washington Quarterly*, vol. 13, no. 1 (Winter 1990), p. 104.
8. Congressional Research Service, *The New Directions Mandate and the Agency for International Development*, reprinted in Subcommittee on Legislation and National Security, U.S. Congress, House, Committee on Government Operations, *AID's Administrative and Management Prob-*

lems in Providing Foreign Economic Assistance, 97th Congress, 1st Session, 1981, p. 230.

9. I owe this insight to Vernon W. Ruttan.

10. Congressional Research Service, "New Directions Mandate," p. 258.

11. Quoted in U.S. Congress, House, Committee on Foreign Affairs, Subcommittee on Africa, *Foreign Assistance Legislation for Fiscal Years 1980–1981,* 96th Congress, 1st session, 13 February 1979, p. 14.

12. U.S. Congress, Committee on Appropriations, *Foreign Assistance and Related Programs for 1983,* part 4, 97th Congress, 2nd session, 1982, p. 184.

13. Department of State, *Sub-Saharan Africa and the United States* (Washington, D.C.: Department of State, 1980), p. 32.

14. U.S. Congress, House, Committee on Foreign Affairs, Subcommittee on Africa, *Foreign Assistance Legislation for Fiscal Years 1988-1989,* part 6, 100th Congress, 1st Session, 1987, p. 22.

15. International Monetary Fund, *Direction of Trade Statistics 1990* (Washington, D.C.: International Monetary Fund, 1990), p. 402.

16. Russell B. Scholl, "The International Investment Position of the United States in 1990," *Survey of Current Business,* vol. 71, no. 6 (June 1991), p. 29. The foreign investment figures do not include South Africa.

17. Ravi Gulhati and Raj Nallari, "Reform of Foreign Aid Policies: The Issue of Inter-Country Allocation in Africa," *World Development,* vol. 16, no. 10 (October 1988), pp. 1175–77.

18. U.S. Congress, House, Frank J. Donatelli, Committee on Foreign Affairs, Subcommittee on Africa, *Economic Policy Initiative for Africa,* 98th Congress, 2nd Session, 1984, p. 12.

19. U.S. Congress, House, statement of Edward L. Saiers, Committee on Foreign Affairs, Subcommittee on Africa, *Foreign Assistance Legislation for Fiscal Years 1990–1991,* Part 6, 101st Congress, 1st Session, 1989, p. 26.

20. Congressional Research Service, "An Overview of U.S. Foreign Aid Programs," reprinted in U.S. Congress, House, Committee on Foreign Affairs, *Background Materials on Foreign Assistance,* 101st Congress, 1st Session, 1989, p. 149.

21. U.S. Congress, House, Committee on Foreign Affairs, *Structural Adjustment in Africa: Insights from the Experiences of Ghana and Senegal,* 101st Congress, 1st session, 1989, p. 2.

22. *Foreign Operations, Export Financing, and Related Programs Appropriations Act, 1991,* PL101-13 (10)(c)(1), in *U.S. Statutes at Large* (Washington, D.C.: Government Printing Office, 1991) p. 104, stat. 2027.

23. All figures in this paragraph are from Development Assistance Committee, *Development Cooperation* (Paris: Organization for Economic Cooperation and Development, 1991), p. 212.

24. Ibid.

25. Wolgin, "Fresh Start in Africa," p. 10 and Joshua Greene, "The External Debt Problem of Sub-Saharan Africa," *International Monetary Fund Staff Papers*, vol. 36, no. 4 (December 1989), pp. 854–55.
26. See Wolgin, "Fresh Start in Africa," pp. 25–26.

Chapter 2

1. Government Accounting Office, *Foreign Assistance: Progress in Implementing the Development Fund for Africa*, GAO/NSIAD-91-127 (Washington, D.C.: United States Government Accounting Office, 1991), p. 21.
2. Gulhati and Nallari, "Reform of Foreign Policies," p. 1177.
3. AID, "FY 1992 Congressional Presentation," reprinted in U.S. Congress, Committee on Appropriations, *Foreign Operations, Export Financing, and Related Programs Appropriations for 1992*, 102nd Congress, 1st session, 1991, pp. 175, 179.
4. See, for instance, Alice Amsden, *Asia's Next Giant: South Korea and Late Industrialization* (New York: Oxford University Press, 1989), p. 4.
5. Paul Glewwe and Kwaku A. Twum-Baah, *The Distribution of Welfare in Ghana, 1987–1988*, Living Standards Measurement Study Working Paper no. 75 (Washington, D.C.: The World Bank, 1991), p. 65.
6. *The New York Times* ("Get the Right Grip on Foreign Aid," June 5, 1991) has advocated aid linked to cuts in military spending. UNICEF has suggested conditionality based on increases in social spending. See UNICEF, *The State of the World's Children, 1991* (Oxford: Oxford University Press, 1991), p. 68.
7. Chalmers Johnson, *MITI and the Japanese Miracle* (Stanford: Stanford University Press, 1982), p. 306.

Chapter 3

1. Fiscal Affairs Department, *Fund-Supported Programs, Fiscal Policy and Income Distribution*, IMF Occasional Paper no. 46 (Washington, D.C.: IMF, 1986), pp. 42–53. Given that fourteen African countries belong to the franc zone and cannot voluntarily change the rate at which their currency trades, a large proportion of the countries that have the flexibility to set their own exchange rate have been asked to devalue.
2. William Jaeger and Charles Humphreys, "The Effect of Policy Reforms on Agricultural Incentives in Sub-Saharan Africa," *American Journal of Agricultural Economics*, vol. 70, no. 5 (December 1988), p. 1037.
3. Simon Commander, "Prices, Markets & Rigidities," in Simon Commander, ed., *Structural Adjustment & Agriculture: Theory & Practice in Africa & Latin America* (London: James Currey, 1989), p. 229.

4. World Bank, *Accelerated Development in Sub-Saharan Africa* (Washington, D.C.: The World Bank, 1981), p. 187.
5. The World Bank is advancing the methodology used to evaluate a country's economic performance. For the most recent effort, see The World Bank, *Adjustment Lending Policies for Sustainable Growth,* Policy and Research Series no. 14 (Washington, D.C.: The World Bank, 1990), pp. 23–25.
6. World Bank, *Africa's Adjustment and Growth in the 1990s* (Washington, D.C.: The World Bank, 1989) and Economic Commission for Africa, *Statistics and Policies* (Addis Ababa: ECA, 1989).
7. Justin B. Zulu and Saleh M. Nsouli, *Adjustment Programs in Africa: The Recent Experience,* IMF Occasional Paper no. 34 (Washington, D.C.: IMF, 1985), p. 27.
8. See World Bank, *Africa's Adjustment and Growth in the 1980s,* 1989, and ECA, *Statistics and Policies,* 1989.
9. World Bank, *Sub-Saharan Africa: From Crisis to Sustainable Growth* (Washington, D.C.: The World Bank, 1989), p. 40.
10. Edward J. Perkins, "The Seedlings of Hope: U.S. Policy in Africa," *Department of State Bulletin,* vol. 89, no. 2149 (August 1989), p. 70.
11. The World Bank, *Adjustment Lending Policies for Sustainable Growth,* p. 17.
12. Ibid., p. 52.
13. Uma Lele, "Agricultural Growth, Domestic Policies, the External Environment and Assistance to Africa: Lessons of a Quarter Century," in Colleen Roberts, ed., *Trade, Aid and Policy Reform: Proceedings of the Eighth Agriculture Sector Symposium* (Washington, D.C.: World Bank, 1988), p. 146.
14. IMF, "Structural Reform in Fund-Supported Programs," in Development Committee, *Problems and Issues in Structural Adjustment,* no. 23 (Washington, D.C.: Development Committee, 1990), p. 6, and World Bank, *Making Adjustment Work for the Poor: A Framework for Policy Reform in Africa* (Washington, D.C.: The World Bank, 1990), p. 1.

Chapter 4

1. IMF, *Government Finance Statistics Yearbook* (Washington, D.C.: IMF, 1990), p. 44.
2. John R. Nellis, *Public Enterprises in Sub-Saharan Africa,* World Bank Discussion Paper no. 1 (Washington, D.C.: World Bank, 1986), p. 17.
3. Ibid., pp. 17–19.
4. W. Adda, "State-Owned Enterprises," mimeo, May 1989, p. 2.
5. Task Force on International Private Enterprise, *Report to the President* (Washington, D.C.: The Task Force, 1984), p. 45.
6. President's Commission on Privatization, *Privatization: Toward More Effective Government* (Washington, D.C.: The Commission, 1988), p. 211.

7. L. Gray Cowan, "A Global Overview of Privatization," in Steve H. Hanke, ed., *Privatization and Development* (California: Institute for Contemporary Studies, 1987), p. 15.

8. See, for instance, Elliot Berg and Mary M. Shirley, *Divestiture in Developing Countries,* World Bank Discussion Paper no. 11 (Washington, D.C.: The World Bank, 1987), p. 4.

9. Don Babai, "The World Bank and the IMF: Rolling Back the State or Backing its Role?" in Raymond Vernon, ed., *The Promise of Privatization* (New York: Council on Foreign Relations, 1988), p. 266.

10. Nigel Harris, *The End of the Third World: Newly Industrializing Countries and the Decline of an Ideology* (London: Penguin Press, 1986), p. 42.

11. Alice H. Amsden, "The State and Taiwan's Economic Development," in Peter B. Evans, Dietrich Rueschemeyer, and Theda Skocpol, eds., *Bringing the State Back In* (Cambridge: Cambridge University Press, 1985), p. 91.

12. The fact that state actions in Asia were usually supportive of the private sector and of exports is usually missed by those in Africa and in the United States who want to use the experience of the newly industrializing countries to legitimate the kind of state intervention that was in the past justified by allegiance to socialism.

13. Giovanni Andrea Cornia, Richard Jolley, and Frances Stewart, eds., *Adjustment with a Human Face,* vol. 1 (Oxford: Clarendon Press, 1987), p. 135.

14. "Aid to Africa: After the Market," *The Economist,* December 8, 1990, p. 48.

15. World Bank, *World Development Report 1992,* p. 219.

16. Interview with author, London, August 20, 1990.

17. E. Oti Boateng et. al., *A Poverty Profile for Ghana, 1987-1988,* Social Dimensions of Adjustment in Sub-Saharan Africa Working Paper no. 5 (Washington, D.C.: The World Bank, 1990), p. 14.

18. Paul Glewwe and Dennis de Tray, *The Poor during Adjustment: A Case Study of Côte d'Ivoire,* Living Standards Measurement Survey Paper no. 47 (Washington, D.C.: The World Bank, 1988), p. 13.

19. Ibid., p. 28.

20. Ibid., p. 15.

21. Ravi Kanbur, *Poverty and the Social Dimensions of Structural Adjustment in Côte d'Ivoire* (Washington, D.C.: The World Bank, 1990), p. 45.

22. That is, the price that would have been determined by supply and demand in a free market.

23. Peter S. Heller et. al., *The Implications of Fund-Supported Adjustment Programs for Poverty: Experiences in Selected Countries,* IMF Occasional Paper no. 58 (Washington, D.C.: IMF, 1988), p. 17.

24. World Bank, *World Development Report 1991,* pp. 218, 274.

Chapter 5

1. World Bank, *World Debt Tables*, vol. 1 (Washington, D.C.: The World Bank, 1991), p. 124.
2. United Nations Development Program and the World Bank, *Africa's Adjustment and Growth in the 1980's* (Washington, D.C.: The World Bank, 1989), p. 17.
3. Reginald Herbold Green, "Comments," in Carol Lancaster and John Williamson, eds., *African Debt and Financing* (Washington, D.C.: Institute for International Economics, 1986), p. 22.
4. United Nations, *World Economic Survey, 1989* (New York: UN, 1989), p. 155.
5. "IMF Toughens Stand on African Arrears," *Africa Recovery*, vol. 4, no. 1 (April–June 1990), p. 3.
6. World Bank, *Financing Adjustment with Growth in Sub-Saharan Africa, 1986–1990* (Washington, D.C.: The World Bank, 1986).
7. World Bank, *World Debt Tables*, vol. 1, pp. 120, 124.
8. Ibid., p. 124 and World Bank, *World Debt Tables*, vol. 2 (Washington, D.C.: The World Bank, 1991), p. 290.
9. World Bank, *World Debt Tables*, vol. 1, pp. 124, 136.
10. "Bush Acts to Ease African Debt," *The New York Times*, July 7, 1989.
11. World Bank, *World Development Report 1990* (Washington, D.C.: The World Bank, 1990), p. 126.
12. Ernest Hasch, "Limited Progress on African Debt," *Africa Recovery*, vol. 4, no. 3–4 (October–December 1990), p. 42.
13. For instance, the World Bank's recent report on poverty noted that Africa was the only region where poverty would increase markedly in the next few years. World Bank, *World Development Report 1990*, p. 5.

Chapter 6

1. World Bank, *Sub-Saharan Africa: From Crisis to Sustained Growth*, p. 60.
2. "Freedom and World Prosperity," State Department Current Policy Document no. 1210 (Washington, D.C.: State Department, 1989), p. 1.
3. The phrase is from Alain Rouquie, *The Military and the State in Latin America* (Berkeley: University of California Press, 1987), pp. 343–4.
4. Claude Welch, *No Farewell to Arms?* (Boulder: Westview Press, 1987), p. 20.
5. Andre Lijphart, *Democracies: Patterns of Majoritarian and Consensus Government in Twenty-One Countries* (New Haven: Yale University Press, 1984), chapters 1, 2.
6. See Atul Kohli, *Democracy and Discontent: India's Growing Crisis of Governability* (Cambridge: Cambridge University Press, 1990).
7. Robert A. Packenham, *Liberal America and the Third World* (Princeton: Princeton University Press, 1973), p. 20.

INDEX

ABOUT THE AUTHOR

Jeffrey Herbst is an Assistant Professor of Politics and International Affairs at Princeton University's Woodrow Wilson School. He was a Fulbright Research Associate at the University of Zimbabwe and received a Robert S. McNamara Post-Doctoral Fellowship to conduct research while at the University of Ghana, Legon. He has published *State Politics in Zimbabwe* and *The Politics of Reform in Ghana, 1982–1991* (both from the University of California Press) and several articles analyzing the dynamics of reform and other aspects of politics in Africa. From 1992 to 1993 Herbst was a Fulbright Visiting Professor at the University of Cape Town and the University of the Western Cape.

7094